Mountain Biking
Santa Cruz

The Ultimate Trail & Ride Guide
for the Santa Cruz Area

David & Allison Diller

E**X**TREMELINE
Productions

All riding for this book was performed on Santa Cruz Bicycles.

WARNING!
Please Read This Important Information!

By nature, mountain biking is a potentially dangerous sport with many risks and unavoidable hazards. As a guide, this book does not replace common sense and sound judgment. Nor is this book able to disclose all of the potential dangers associated with riding and with the trails depicted. All the readers and users of this book must accept the inevitable risks involved and assume complete responsibility for their own actions and safety.

While considerable effort has been made to provide accurate information, there may be accidental omissions or errors. The authors, publishers, editors, contributors, and distributors accept no liability for any mistakes, errors, changes in policy, trail closures or re-routes, trail conditions, or for any injuries, deaths, losses, and other relevant factors. By purchasing and/or utilizing this book, the consumer accepts full responsibility for its use.

Please use caution on the trails, read signs, and check the current policy on trail-use before riding. Always use proper safety and protective gear when mountain biking.

Table of Contents

Singletrack riding in Santa Cruz.

Welcome to Santa Cruz!

Get stoked! This west-coast mecca of mountain biking has year-round riding with a variety of insane terrain and gorgeous scenery. Containing more state parks than any other county, Santa Cruz offers one of the most varied and beautiful coastal environments on the planet. From the surf to the mountains, you can bike an abundance of trails in redwood forests, through grasslands, on coastal cliffs, and beside pristine creeks. Get ready to ride roller coaster singletrack, bomb fast and furious fire roads, test your skills on technical trails, or simply cruise the many rides. There are plenty of options for all ability levels whether you want a scenic family ride or a gnarly downhill technical challenge. It is no wonder that Bike Magazine has declared Santa Cruz both a "mecca," and a "mountain biking paradise" with "incredible trails."

Mountain biking in Santa Cruz will not only thrill you, it will get you pumped on life! You will find yourself completely immersed in nature; whether in a giant redwood grove or viewing massive surf as you ride down the coastal mountain grasslands. The abundance of wildlife will often add an exhilarating surprise to anyone's ride! Be prepared; mountain biking here is an incredible experience.

About This Guidebook

The Book
This pocket-sized guide is meant to be as transportable and versatile as you. While providing all the necessary information about mountain biking in Santa Cruz, it will aid you in choosing and locating the appropriate trails and rides for your cycling adventure.

This book is categorized into sections by specific areas and parks. In each section, an introduction is given and the particular rides of the area are depicted. Accurately detailed maps and elevation profiles are provided for each ride. In addition, a "Trail Guide" section, which compares and details specific trails, is provided for many of the state parks that have a myriad of riding choices. This enables you, the biker, to have the freedom and ability to piece together your own perfect ride.

Map Legend

– – – – – – – – –	SINGLETRACK
....	NO BIKES TRAIL
= = = = = = = = = =	FIRE ROAD
==============	GRADED DIRT ROAD
═══════════	PAVED ROAD
═══════════	MAIN PAVED ROAD
▬▬▬▬▬▬▬▬	HIGHWAY
+++++++++++++++++++	TRAIN TRACKS
— ·· — ·· — ·· — ·· —	PROPERTY BOUNDARY
——— ··· ——— ··· ———	RIVER OR CREEK

▲	NORTH ARROW	↙	RIDE DIRECTION
ⓟ	RIDE PARKING	△	CAMPING AREA
Ⓟ	OTHER PARKING	▪■	BUILDINGS
★	RIDE START	⌂	RESTROOM
⚘	PICNIC AREA	•—•	GATE

Ratings and Ride Details

Location: General area of the ride.

Distance: Measured in miles.

Elevation: Depicts the minimum and maximum elevation you will encounter on the ride.

Trail Surface: Explains what kind of trail you'll be riding.

Type of Ride: Defines the ride either as a Loop, Out & Back, or One-Way.

Terrain: Tells you about the surrounding environment and scenery of the ride.

Technical Level: Describes how difficult the trail is to bike, relative to other Santa Cruz trails.

Easy: Usually a mostly smooth wide dirt road.

Medium: Some roots, ruts, rocks, and/or potholes with some maneuvering involved; usually on a tighter trail.

Difficult: Narrow trail with more roots, ruts, drop-offs, and/or rocks; steep sections.

Most Difficult: Steeper and rougher sections, obstacles, frequent changes in gradient; hike-n-bike likely in some sections.

Exertion Level: The general aerobic level of a ride.

Mild: For the most part, the ride is flat with little or no climbing.

Moderate: Hills with some gradual or short steep climbs.

Strenuous: Longer and steeper uphill sections that might get you panting.

Very Strenuous: Heart pounding, mega uphill sections.

Highlights: A brief description of the main features of the ride to get you pumped!

Options: Ways to lengthen, shorten, or add variety to the ride. Helps the rider to customize the rides.

Note: Anything that may be noteworthy on the ride.

Directions/Access: Specific directions to the trailhead. When mileage is given from Santa Cruz, it refers specifically to the intersection of Highway 17 and Highway 1 unless otherwise specified.

Ride Profile: This graph depicts the ride in terms of elevation gain and loss related to mileage - so you know what to expect. The major changes in elevation and key features are shown. Please keep in mind that the scope of the profiles may require that quick changes in elevation be left out. Because of the variety in the elevation and the length of different rides depicted, exact comparisons between profiles can not be made without taking these factors into account.

Mileage Guide: Provides key features and a descri ption of the ride to prevent you from getting lost. These are labeled in miles for those with either bike computers or mathematically gifted minds.

Index of Rides by Category
Use this index as a reference tool to pick out what kind of ride you prefer; whether it be Sweet Singletrack, Mellow Cruisers, Technical Tests, Hammerhead Climbs, Insane Downhills, Epic Big-Day Rides, Multi-Interest Rides, Quick Fixes, Multi-Park/Interregional Rides, or Santa Cruz Classics. (Page 180).

Santa Cruz Climate

Santa Cruz offers good year round riding conditions. While the overall climate is mild, occasionally it will be significantly colder and rainier in winter. Summer is not always hot either; cold fog and breezes near the coast can make it quite chilly. At the same time, the inland areas may be very hot and "Indian summers" can warm the whole coastal region late in the year. If you are unsure of the weather, it is best to be prepared for any situation by wearing layers.

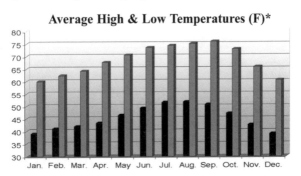

Average High & Low Temperatures (F)*

Average Total Precipitation (inches)*

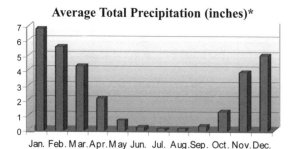

*Period of Record: 7/1/1948 to 12/31/2000; Data from Western Regional Climate Center; www.rcc.dri.edu

Monthly Sunrise Times (standard time)**

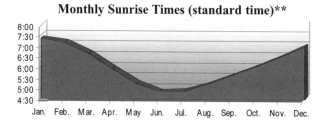

Monthly Sunset Times (standard time)**

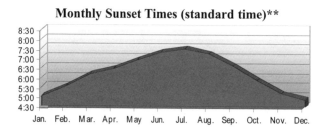

**Times are in Standard Time. Add 1 hour for Day Light Savings Time (DST). DST starts at 2 AM on the first Sunday in April, and ends 2 AM on the last Sunday in October.

Other Considerations

The following considerations are nothing to stress about, but it helps to be aware of them while riding in Santa Cruz.

Poison Oak

Beware! Santa Cruz has an abundance of poison oak, particularly near creeks and moist forested areas. Try to avoid touching it as you mountain bike around Santa Cruz!

Stinging Nettles

These plants are also abundant near creeks. Instantly you'll know what they are if you brush up against this plant. Don't worry! The sting goes away!

Ticks

Watch out for these annoying little pests in the brush, especially in early Spring. Its wise to check yourself periodically, especially if you find yourself bailing out in the bushes! Twisting with tweezers should do the job.

Mountain Lions

Mountain lions have been reported in all of the local parks, although it is very rare to see one. Consider yourself privileged if you spot one! However, it is obviously important to be extremely cautious around them.

Renegade Trails

Santa Cruz seems to be well known for many of its illegal, closed, or renegade trails. Despite the fact that most of these trails are either on private property, for hiking only, or are closed for environmental and other reasons; they sometimes get ridden simply because they are great singletrack trails. However, riding illegal trails often hurts the overall mountain biking community by causing even more trail closures.

If you would like to see more singletrack opened to the public, become involved politically by contacting elected officials and joining a mountain bike advocacy group such as Mountain Bikers of Santa Cruz (www.mbosc.org). As more mountain bikers voice their opinions, politicians and park officials will listen. While the authors would absolutely love to see more singletrack open to bikers, this book strongly encourages bikers to respect the laws and ride the many "open" trails.

When non-biking or closed trails are mentioned and/or shown on maps in this book, it is for the purpose of identifying your location in respect to the other trails that you may see in the area. Please do not ride these trails.

Mountain Biking Ethics

IMBA'S Trail Rules:

Thousands of miles of dirt trails have been closed to mountain bicyclists. The irresponsible riding habits of a few riders have been a factor. Do your part to maintain trail access by observing the following rules of the trail, formulated by IMBA, the International Mountain Bicycling Association. IMBA's mission is to promote environmentally sound and socially responsible mountain bicycling.

RIDE ON OPEN TRAILS ONLY. Respect trail and road closures (ask if not sure), avoid possible trespass on private land, obtain permits or other authorization as may be required. Federal and state Wilderness areas are closed to cycling. The way you ride will influence trail management decisions and policies.

LEAVE NO TRACE. Be sensitive to the dirt beneath you. Even on open (legal) trails, you should not ride under conditions where you will leave evidence of your passing, such as on certain soils after a rain. Recognize different types of soils and trail construction; practice low-impact cycling. This also means staying on existing trails and not creating new ones. Don't cut switchbacks. Be sure to pack out at least as much as you pack in.

CONTROL YOUR BICYCLE! Inattention for even a second can cause problems. Obey all bicycle speed regulations and recommendations.

ALWAYS YIELD TRAIL. Make known your approach well in advance. A friendly greeting or bell is considerate and works well; don't startle others. Show your respect when passing by slowing to a walking pace or even stopping. Anticipate other trail users around corners or in blind spots.

NEVER SPOOK ANIMALS. All animals are startled by an unannounced approach, a sudden movement, or a loud noise. This can be dangerous for you, others, and the animals. Give animals extra room and time to adjust to you. When passing horses use special care and follow directions from the horseback riders (ask if uncertain). Running cattle and disturbing wildlife is a serious offense. Leave gates as you found them, or as marked.

PLAN AHEAD. Know your equipment, your ability, and the area in which you are riding — and prepare accordingly. Be self-sufficient at all times, keep your equipment in good repair, and carry necessary supplies for changes in weather or other conditions. A well-executed trip is a satisfaction to you and not a burden or offense to others. Always wear a helmet and appropriate safety gear.

KEEP TRAILS OPEN BY SETTING A GOOD EXAMPLE OF ENVIRONMENTALLY SOUND AND SOCIALLY RESPONSIBLE OFF-ROAD CYCLING.

Author's Trail Rules:

Do unto others as you would want them to do unto you. Being a jerk is not cool; instead yield to everyone on the trail and help those in need. Use common sense and respect all of God's creation for your enjoyment and for all those who follow. Always be joyful and have lots of fun!

Wilder Ranch State Park

Wilder Ranch's Old Cabin Trail.

If you've been yearning for one big bike park with dazzling terrain and mind-bending vistas close to town; Wilder Ranch is the bomb!

Whatever you desire; singletrack, fire roads, open meadows, forest, creeks, coastal terraces, valleys, ocean views, dirt, rocks, sand…its all just north of Santa Cruz waiting to be ridden! Containing almost 40 miles of multi-use trails throughout 6,000 acres, Wilder Ranch (including the addition of Gray

Whale Ranch) is a mecca for California mountain biking. Undoubtedly, all devout mountain biking pilgrims eventually find themselves ritually exploring the extensive network of trails.

Views, singletrack, sun...welcome to Wilder Ranch.

Once a prospering dairy operation and a major practice spot for the rodeo circuit, Wilder Ranch is now active with a 22-acre historical ranch complex. This Cultural Preserve also provides evidence of Native American habitation and a Spanish mission adobe building. In addition, cattle grazing and agriculture are still found in the area.

Wilder Ranch is located just a couple miles north of Santa Cruz off of Highway 1. The park is open for mountain biking between 8 AM and sunset.

Part of the Wilder Ranch Cultural Preserve.

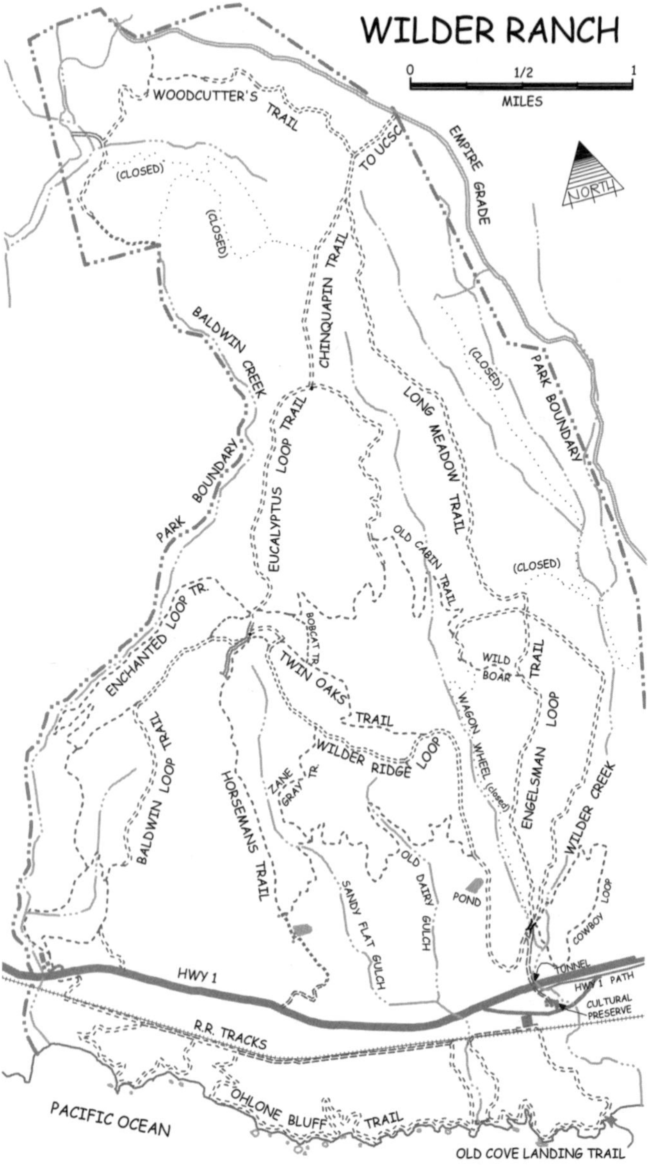

WILDER RANCH

0   1/2   1
MILES

NORTH

WOODCUTTER'S TRAIL

TO UCSC

EMPIRE GRADE

(CLOSED)

(CLOSED)

CHINQUAPIN TRAIL

PARK BOUNDARY

BALDWIN CREEK

PARK BOUNDARY

(CLOSED)

LONG MEADOW TRAIL

EUCALYPTUS LOOP TRAIL

OLD CABIN TRAIL

(CLOSED)

ENCHANTED LOOP TR.

BOBCAT TR.

TWIN OAKS TRAIL

WILD BOAR TRAIL

WAGON WHEEL (CLOSED)

ENGELSMAN LOOP

WILDER RIDGE LOOP

BALDWIN LOOP TRAIL

ZANE GRAY TR.

HORSEMANS TRAIL

OLD DAIRY GULCH

POND

WILDER CREEK

SANDY FLAT GULCH

COWBOY LOOP

TUNNEL

HWY 1 PATH

CULTURAL PRESERVE

HWY 1

R.R. TRACKS

PACIFIC OCEAN

OHLONE BLUFF TRAIL

OLD COVE LANDING TRAIL

Ride 1
Old Cove Landing/Ohlone Bluff Trail

A snap shot of the natural wonders to be enjoyed while biking Old Cove Landing and Ohlone bluff.

Location: Two miles north of Western Dr in Santa Cruz.

Distance: 1-14 miles roundtrip.

Elevation: 0/50 ft.

Trail Surface: 23% wide trail; 77% dirt road & doubletrack.

Type of Ride: Out & back.

Terrain: Ocean cliffs; grasslands; beaches; agriculture area.

Technical Level: Easy; a mildly technical section involves descending a beach cliff area, crossing beach, and climbing back up at Old Cove. There is also an option to ride around the cove, rather than descending to the beach.

Exertion Level: Mild; almost completely flat.

Highlights: This is an incredibly beautiful ride along some of the most pristine coastline in California. You'll pass several coves, deserted beaches, and rock outcroppings. Keep your eyes open for wildlife; seals, sea lions, dolphins, whales, birds, bobcats, and much more! Particularly awe-inspiring when there are large waves, this is a "must-do" Santa Cruz ride for any level biker!

Options: Most people ride this as an out & back and simply turn around when they feel like it. A much longer ride is possible with the addition of the other inland Wilder Ranch trails, such as the Baldwin Loop Trail.

Note: Be prepared: since this ride is right on the ocean, it can occasionally be breezy and cool along the trail even in mid-summer. Also, note that there are many farm roads on the inland side. At some points in the ride, the trail merges with these roads as you pass around the larger coves.

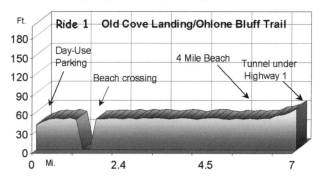

Directions/Access: In Santa Cruz, take Highway 1 North through town (Mission St). About 2 miles from the outskirts of town, turn left into Wilder Ranch State Park when you see the brown sign on the right. To enter the parking lot, pass through the entrance booth. The day-use parking will be on the right and costs $5. Alternative free parking is in the dirt pull-outs on Highway 1, but don't leave valuables in the car there! If you are riding from town, take the paved bike path that parallels Highway 1 (see Ride 32).

Mileage Guide	
0.0	From the information panel near the parking lot and restrooms, head toward the beach by taking the dirt trail just ahead. It is labeled "Old Cove Landing Trail." Soon, you will merge left onto the dirt road/path.

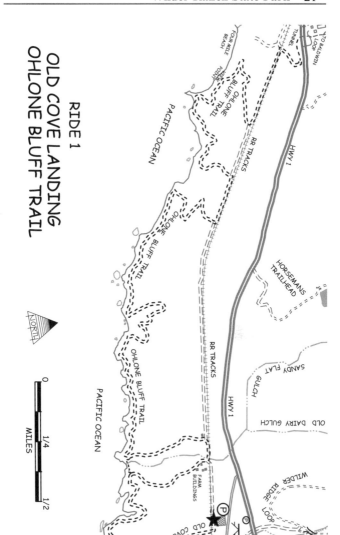

RIDE 1
OLD COVE LANDING
OHLONE BLUFF TRAIL

.1	Cross over train tracks here.
.6	On the left is a viewing platform and information panel overlooking Wilder Beach. The ride will stay along the cliffs for the most part now. Keep your eyes open for natural bridges, ocean life, birds, bobcats, etc.
1.3	Keep to the left as the trail merges with the dirt road around the cove.
1.6	You'll reach a large cove now. A steep trail goes down the cliff, across the beach, and continues up the opposite cliff to the other side. This will put you at Mile 2.5 on this Mileage Guide. If the tide is too high or you would rather not carry your bike, there is another option. You may continue on the dirt road inland to get around the cove.
2.0	As you ride inland, you will enter a farm equipment area with a state park sign; go straight and pass through the area. Then turn left and ride along the train tracks.
2.2	From the tracks, veer left up a short hill. Just before you reach the shed, make a sharp left to head back toward the ocean on a grassy doubletrack.
2.5	Soon you will be back on the cliffs! On the left, the beach trail merges. The trail/doubletrack is now less maintained with more potholes and puddles, depending on the season. Continue along the cliffs.
4.8	You'll come to railroad tracks again. Just before the tracks, go left and ride along the side of them.
5.1	Go left and head back toward the beach.
5.9	Watch out for seasonal sand traps!
6.0	Off to the left, you can peak at 4-Mile Beach through the trees. From this scenic place, you'll often see surfers shredding up the waves! Most people opt to ride back from this point. To keep riding to the Baldwin Loop, continue on around the cove as you pass brussel sprouts on the inland side.

6.3	The trail merges with a farm road again. Keep left.
6.5	Stay straight through the 3-way split.
6.7	Intersection! Left goes down to 4-Mile Beach. To reach the tunnel under Highway 1 and the Baldwin Loop, go right across the tracks. Ahead, you'll see a sign for "Baldwin Loop Trail" and a split in the trail; take either.
6.8	As you are heading toward the highway, turn left on a beat-up asphalt road.
6.9	Veer left off of paved road onto the posted singletrack.
7.0	You've reached the tunnel. Continuing on will take you up the Baldwin Loop Trail (Ride 6A). Otherwise turn around and head back.

A section of doubletrack on the Ohlone Bluffs.

Ride 2
Wilder Ridge Loop

The "Dairy Mill Trail" section of the Wilder Ridge Loop.

Location: Off of Highway 1, just north of Santa Cruz.

Distance: 8.2 miles.

Elevation: 25/630 ft.

Trail Surface: 46% singletrack; 54% fire road.

Type of Ride: Loop.

Terrain: Coastal grasslands; sparse forest; ridges.

Technical Level: Medium/Difficult; some steep and rocky sections.

Exertion Level: Moderate/Strenuous; lots of climbing at first but its mostly gradual.

Highlights: Besides exhibiting insane views, this ride rates high on the fun factor! Most of the climbing is on a fire road exposed to nonstop panoramic ocean vistas, while the descent is on exhilarating singletrack. The "Dairy Mill Trail" section is a superb winding singletrack, and the "Horseman's Trail" section will thrill those who love steep descents.

Options: Combine with other Wilder or Gray Whale Trails to lengthen the ride. Zane Gray Trail is also a great singletrack option that bisects the Loop for a shorter ride.

Note: Remember to walk bikes through the Cultural Preserve.

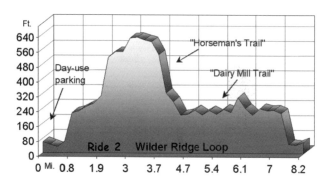

Directions/Access: See Directions/Access on Ride 1.

Mileage Guide	
0.0	From the Wilder Ranch day-use parking area, head from the bathrooms downhill on the paved road.
.15	Turn left at the Cultural Preserve and walk your bikes through this area toward the tunnel.
.30	Tunnel.
.45	At the split, after passing the information panel, go left up Wilder Ridge Loop (there will be a signpost up on the left).
1.2	Continue climbing straight ahead (right) at the Wilder Ridge Loop split.
2.0	Split. Twin Oaks Trail takes off on the right. This option can be taken if you prefer to climb singletrack (this will put you just above the Mile 3.2 turnoff on this Mileage Guide). Otherwise, grunt up this next steep section.

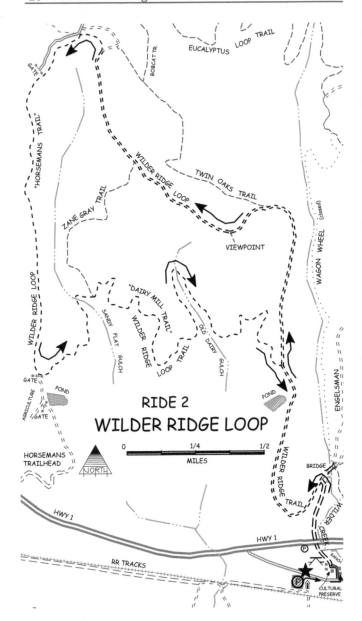

RIDE 2
WILDER RIDGE LOOP

2.2	Just to the left is an awesome place to relieve lactic-acid-filled legs; views of all of Santa Cruz and Monterey Bay! To continue, stay on the main trail through a much flatter section.
2.7	Pass Zane Gray Trail on the left.
3.2	Look for the singletrack shortcut trail on the left. Take this to get to the singletrack section of Wilder Ridge Loop known as "Horseman's Trail."
3.3	Just before you reach the sign post at the paved road, veer left on the singletrack that will parallel the road (toward the ocean) for a while. As you descend the ridge, you'll likely hear noises from the landfill on the right.
4.6	Just after you pass horse corrals, the trail makes a left.
4.7	Keep to the left as you ride into the fabulous section of singletrack known as the Dairy Mill Trail. On the right is an alternate access to Highway 1 through the gate. (If you ever take this, open the gate and ride left on the farm road .1 mile. On the left there are 2 gates; take the rightmost/farthest one and head along the grassy road to Highway 1).
5.2	Zane Gray Trail merges on the left. Keep riding straight.
7.0	Go right as you reach the dirt road section of the Wilder Ridge Loop.
7.7	Merge right onto the dirt road.
7.9	Pass under the bridge and walk your bike through the Cultural Preserve to get back to the parking area.
8.2	End of the line.

Ride 3
Baldwin/Enchanted Loop

Cruising through the lush Enchanted Loop forest.

Location: 4 miles north of Santa Cruz on Highway 1.

Distance: 5.3 miles.

Elevation: 30/580 ft.

Trail Surface: 79% singletrack; 21% fire road & doubletrack.

Type of Ride: Loop.

Terrain: Coastal grasslands; forest; rocks; creeks; views.

Technical Level: Medium/Difficult.

Aerobic Level: Moderate/Strenuous.

Highlights: Sweet uncrowded singletrack sections, great workout, fun downhill segments, ocean and canyon views, wildlife; this ride has it all! However, the lowest section on the Baldwin Loop can sometimes become very overgrown in the summer. It all depends on how many people are riding it and doing trail maintenance.

Options: There are plenty of trails in Wilder that can be added to lengthen your ride. For a quicker ride, bike only the Baldwin Loop.

Note: The Enchanted Loop Trail is often closed after major rain storms due to erosion problems.

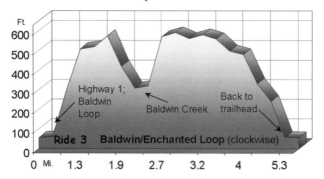

Directions/Access: In Santa Cruz, take Highway 1 North (Mission St) past the main entrance to Wilder Ranch. Park at the 4-Mile beach parking area near the highway tunnel. The trailhead is just beyond the tunnel on the inland side. An alternative is to park in the dirt pullout just before mail box # 3810 on Highway 1. Go down the paved road past the gate and spot the trailhead just ahead on right.

Mileage Guide	
0.0	The main trailhead, signed " Baldwin Loop Trail," is just down from the tunnel near a ranch/house area on the left.
.10	Go left when the Baldwin Loop splits. This will take you into a lush canyon on smooth singletrack. Enjoy your easy breathing now; the trail steepens dramatically ahead.
.60	Pass the Eagle Cutoff trail.
1.0	Rocky section. Just ahead the trail mellows from its steep gradient. Soon you'll see a spectacular canyon off to the left.

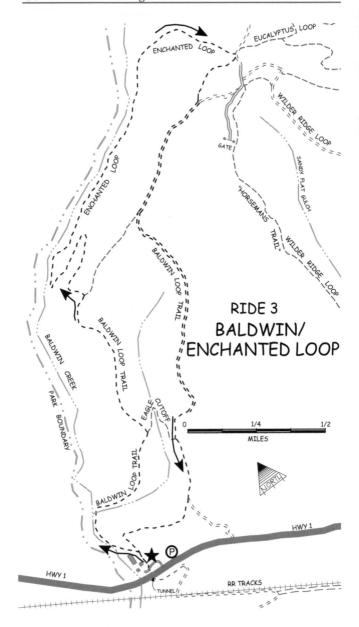

EUCALYPTUS LOOP

ENCHANTED LOOP

WILDER RIDGE LOOP

ENCHANTED LOOP

GATE

SANDY FLAT GULCH

"HORSEMANS" TRAIL"

WILDER RIDGE LOOP

BALDWIN LOOP TRAIL

RIDE 3
BALDWIN/
ENCHANTED LOOP

BALDWIN LOOP TRAIL

BALDWIN CREEK

PARK BOUNDARY

EAGLE CUTOFF

0   1/4   1/2
MILES

NORTH

BALDWIN LOOP TRAIL

HWY 1

HWY 1

P

RR TRACKS

TUNNEL

1.6	After the trail plateaus, the Baldwin Loop intersects with the Enchanted Loop. Stay to the left and merge onto the Enchanted Trail. The first .2 miles of this super fun section are more technical; steep, rutted and rooted. Then you will hit some smooth fast singletrack through a mossy fern and redwood forest.
2.2	Stay straight as the trail parallels Baldwin Creek.
2.4	There will be a steep uphill as you reemerge from the forest. Keep you eyes open for wildlife in this hotspot as you crank up through the fields ahead!
2.8	You will emerge at the old corral area. The Enchanted Loop splits here; both sections are to the right. Take the immediate singletrack on the right that leads back into the forest.
3.0	Merge right onto the Enchanted fire road, which winds through open meadows with broad vistas.
3.5	Stay left at this split and descend the other side of Baldwin Loop. (Right takes you back to the Enchanted Loop). The next section on Baldwin has plenty of variety; doubletrack, dirt road, singletrack, rocky sections, amazing ocean views, and plenty of speed.
4.5	Pass Eagle Cutoff Trail on the right.
4.8	As 4-Mile beach comes into view, there will be a split. Go right on the singletrack.
5.3	Back at the trailhead.

Baldwin Trailhead.

Ride 4
Wilder Singletrack Loop

Panorama seascape on the Zane Gray Trail.

Location: Off of Highway 1, just north of Santa Cruz.

Distance: 12.4 miles.

Elevation: 30/630 ft.

Trail Surface: 80% singletrack; 20% fire road.

Type of Ride: Loop.

Terrain: Grasslands; forest; creeks; ocean & mountain views.

Technical Level: Moderate/Difficult; some sections are steep, rocky, rutted, and/or rooted.

Exertion Level: Moderate/Strenuous; lots of changes in elevation, but most of it is gradual.

Highlights: This go-gonzo ride is one way to maximize much of the singletrack ridden in Wilder Ranch. With lots of variety and challenge, it combines Englesman, Wild Boar, Old Cabin, Eucalyptus, Enchanted loop, Twin Oaks, Zane Grey, and Dairy

Mill section of Wilder Ridge Loop. Whoohooo!

Options: Almost endless; add or subtract trails or ride different directions. To lengthen the ride, adding the "Horseman's" section of Wilder Ridge loop or Baldwin Loop are great single-track options.

Note: Yeah, there's more singletrack around, but much of it is off limits for restoration purposes. Please respect the rules when you see a closure sign!

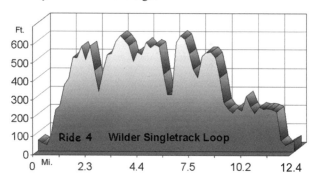

Directions/Access: See Directions/Access on Ride 1.

Mileage Guide	
0.0	From the Wilder Ranch day-use parking, head down the paved road past the restrooms.
.10	Turn left at the Cultural Preserve and walk your bikes through this area toward the tunnel.
.25	Ride under the tunnel past the information panel.
.45	Keep riding straight as you pedal by the Wilder Ridge Loop turnoffs and the corral.
.55	After crossing over the bridge, you'll be at an intersection with the Englesman Loop Trails. Take the leftmost side of the Englesman Loop.
1.8	Time for some singletrack! Go left at the posted sign on Wild Boar Trail.

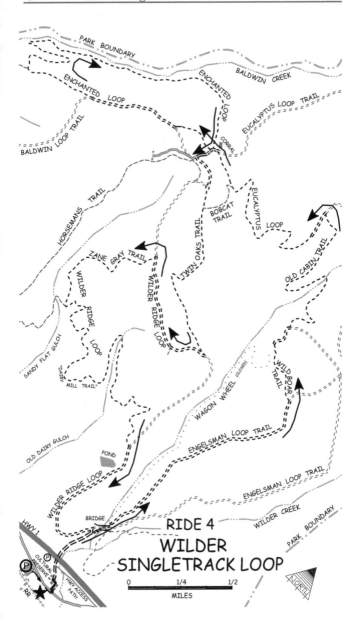

PARK BOUNDARY

BALDWIN CREEK

ENCHANTED LOOP

ENCHANTED LOOP

EUCALYPTUS LOOP TRAIL

BALDWIN LOOP TRAIL

CORRAL

HORSEMANS TRAIL

EUCALYPTUS LOOP

BOBCAT TRAIL

ZANE GRAY TRAIL

TWIN OAKS TRAIL

WILDER RIDGE LOOP

OLD CABIN TRAIL

WILDER RIDGE LOOP

SANDY FLAT GULCH

"DAIRY MILL TRAIL"

WAGON WHEEL (CLOSED)

WILD BOAR TRAIL

OLD DAIRY GULCH

POND

ENGELSMAN LOOP TRAIL

WILDER RIDGE LOOP

ENGELSMAN LOOP TRAIL

BRIDGE

WILDER CREEK

PARK BOUNDARY

HWY 1

CULTURAL PRESERVE

HWY ACCESS PATH

RIDE 4
WILDER
SINGLETRACK LOOP

0   1/4   1/2

MILES

NORTH

2.0	Keep riding as the trail widens and curves up to the right. On the left, you will pass the Wagon Wheel trailhead (closed at the time of press).
2.3	Take a left to descend into the forest on some sweet singletrack; Old Cabin Trail.
3.4	Go left on Eucalyptus Loop Trail.
4.3	Soon you'll come to a split after the second creek crossing; keep going straight (right).
4.6	As you come to the end of the trail, keep going straight into the old corral area. Spot the Enchanted Loop trails just ahead to the right of the dirt road. To ride the loop clockwise, pass the first trail on the right and take the second higher trail that leads into the forest.
4.8	Veer right as you merge onto the Enchanted fire road. More incredible views are just ahead!
5.3	At the split, go to the right on the Enchanted Loop. (Here, the Enchanted loop tangents the Baldwin Loop). At the next split stay to the right again and get ready to rock 'n' roll through this rippin' section of trail!
6.1	As you emerge from the forest, keep your eyes open for wildlife while you power up through the steep field area ahead!
6.5	Back at the old corral area. Turn right and ride up the dirt road (which soon becomes paved).
6.6	Turn left onto the Wilder Ridge fire road.
6.8	How about some more downhill bliss?! If you're into that, go left onto Twin Oaks Trail.
7.1	Ignore Bobcat trail merging on the left.
7.8	Turn right. Hopefully, that descent refreshed you enough to ride up this very steep (but short) section of the Wilder Ridge Loop.
8.0	You might want to catch your breathe at the viewpoint on the left. Otherwise, keep riding up the main trail.
8.5	Zane Gray Trail. Go left on this delightful trail. It will be smooth at first then steep, rocky, and a little rutted.

9.4	Merge left onto the meandering Dairy Mill Trail (part of Wilder Ridge Loop Trail).
11.2	Go right at the Wilder Ridge fire road.
11.9	Merge right onto the dirt road.
12.1	Ride through the tunnel and walk your bike within the ranch complex to get back to the parking area.
12.4	Main parking lot.

Riding up the Englesman Loop Trail.

Ride 5
Wilder-Gray Whale Ride

Location: Just north of Santa Cruz off Highway 1.

Distance: 10-14 miles.

Elevation: 20/1130 ft.

Trail Surface: 100% fire roads & doubletrack. Additional singletrack with the Woodcutter Trail option.

Type of Ride: Loop; with optional out & back section.

Terrain: Grasslands, forested canyons, great views.

Riding Long Meadow Trail near the Lime Kiln area.

Technical Level: Medium; a few sections are steep and may be rutted.

Exertion Level: Strenuous; although a mostly gradual climb.

Highlights: This very scenic loop ride winds throughout much of Wilder and Gray Whale Ranches! Treating you to many beautiful views and varying terrain, this ride includes Wilder Ridge Loop Trail, Eucalyptus Loop Trail, Chinquapin Road, Long Meadow Trail, Englesman Loop Trail, and a possible out & back section on Woodcutter's Trail.

Options: Tons of Options! Substitute sections of the ride for any of the other trails in the area, or pedal it counter-clockwise.

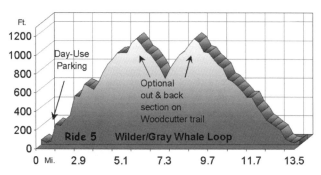

Note: Have fun!

Directions/Access: See Directions/Access on Ride 1.

Mileage Guide	
0.0	From the Wilder Ranch day-use parking area, head from the bathrooms downhill on the paved road.
.15	Turn left at the farm buildings and walk your bikes.
.30	Pass through the tunnel.
.45	Take the first major left to head up the Wilder Ridge Loop Trail.
1.3	Continue climbing straight ahead on the main fire road.
2.0	As you pass Twin Oaks Trail, you'll encounter one of the steepest uphill sections of the ride.
2.2	An awesome viewpoint of all of Santa Cruz and Monterey Bay is off to the left. If you've already caught your breath, keep on the main trail (to the right). Soon you will also pass the Zane Gray Trail off to the left.
3.2	Just ahead, you will pass the top of Twin Oaks Trail as the road curves to the left.
3.4	At the short section of old pavement, turn right and head downhill.
3.5	As the pavement ends, you'll pass by the Enchanted Loop trails off to the left. Stay on the road as it curves around. Soon you'll come to the Eucalyptus Loop; stay on the main fire road here (to the left of the Eucalyptus singletrack trail).
4.7	After the climb, vast expanses of beauty await you! Check out the ocean view through the Eucalyptus grove on your right. To keep riding, take a left through the open gate onto the Chinquapin Trail.
5.6	Decision time: You can turn right onto Long Meadow trail and begin your descent back down. Or, you can extend your ride farther into Gray Whale Ranch on Woodcutter's Trail by riding about 4 more miles total.

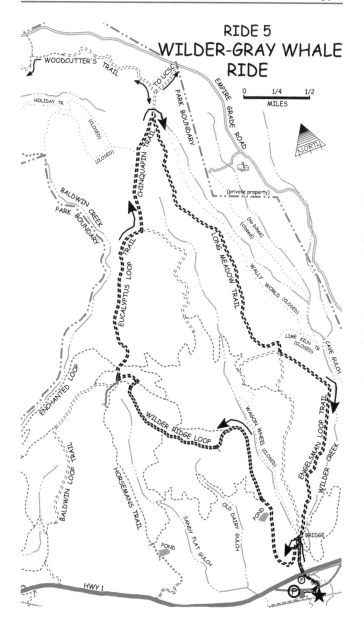

RIDE 5
WILDER-GRAY WHALE
RIDE

WOODCUTTER'S TRAIL

TO UCSC

PARK BOUNDARY

EMPIRE GRADE ROAD

0   1/4   1/2
MILES

NORTH

HOLIDAY TR

(CLOSED)

(CLOSED)

(private property)

BALDWIN CREEK
PARK BOUNDARY

CHINQUAPIN TRAIL

EUCALYPTUS LOOP TRAIL

LONG MEADOW TRAIL

(no bikes)
(closed)

WALLY WORLD (CLOSED)

LIME KILN TR
(CLOSED)

CAVE GULCH

ENCHANTED LOOP

WILDER RIDGE LOOP

WAGON WHEEL (CLOSED)

ENGELSMAN LOOP TRAIL

WILDER CREEK

BALDWIN LOOP TRAIL

HORSEMANS TRAIL

SANDY FLAT GULCH

OLD DAIRY GULCH

POND

POND

BRIDGE

POND

HWY 1

P

P

	(Woodcutter's section is an out & back that descends to a creek and contains some singletrack. It branches off Chinquapin in about .2 miles on the left). Either way, Long Meadow Trail is an exhilarating downhill section!
7.8	Toward the bottom of Long Meadow, stay to the right as the trail splits near the ruins of the old quarry.
7.9	After passing the ruins, you will come to a major 4-way intersection. Ride left onto Englesman Loop.
9.4	As you reach the end of Englesman, merge straight onto the main Wilder dirt road that leads back to the tunnel.
9.7	Tunnel.
10	After passing through the Cultural Preserve, you should be back at the main parking lot.

Appreciating some singletrack on Woodcutter's Trail.

Rides 6 A-O
Wilder/Gray Whale Trail Guide

6A. Baldwin Loop Trail

Distance: 3.5 miles.

Elevation: 30/580 ft.

Trail Surface: 75% singletrack; 25% fire road.

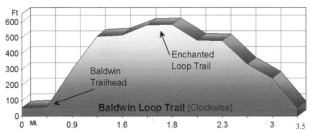

Terrain: Coastal terraces; grasslands; rocks; oaks.

Technical Level: Difficult; some steep parts and ruts.

Exertion Level: Moderate with a Strenuous section; some steep climbs in the beginning.

Highlights: An uncrowded short singletrack loop with unreal ocean and canyon views and a fun fast downhill!

6B. Eagle Cutoff Trail

Distance: .25 miles.

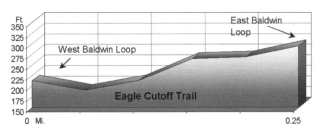

Elevation: 190/290 ft.

Trail Surface: 100% singletrack.

Terrain: Open coastal terrace; gully.

Technical Level: Medium.

Exertion Level: Moderate.

Highlights: Dives into a gully to either side of the Baldwin Loop.

6C. Enchanted Loop Trail

Distance: 2 miles.

Elevation: 330/600 ft.

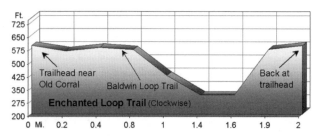

Trail Surface: 73% singletrack; 27% fire road.

Terrain: Coastal grasslands; forest; creek.

Technical Level: Difficult; a few sections are steep with roots, ruts, and small drop-offs.

Exertion Level: Moderate; relatively short but has a steep uphill climb.

Highlights: Short loop with an insane singletrack section through the "Enchanted Forest!" This section is very cool! This trail is often closed during the rainy season and may be partially re-routed soon.

6D. Englesman Loop Trail

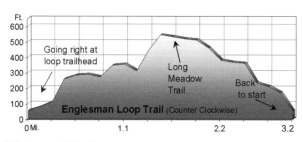

Distance: 3.2 miles.

Elevation: 50/545 ft.

Trail Surface: 100% narrow fire road.

Terrain: Coastal Grasslands with forested canyons.

Technical Level: Easy/Medium.

Exertion Level: Moderate/Strenuous; steady climbing.

Highlights: A pleasant ride with great panoramic ocean views; heads inland and accesses many other trails in Wilder and Gray Whale.

6E. Wild Boar Trail

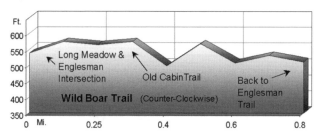

Distance: .8 miles.

Elevation: 510/575 ft.

Trail Surface: 40% singletrack; 60% fire road.

Terrain: Sparse forest.

Technical Level: Easy/Medium.

Exertion Level: Moderate; some climbing.

Highlights: Connects Englesman Loop, Long Meadow Trail, Wagon Wheel Trail, and Old Cabin Trail.

6F. Old Cabin Trail

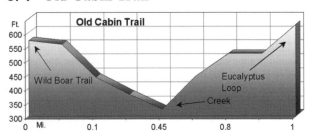

Distance: 1 mile.

Elevation: 325/630 ft.

Trail Surface: 100% singletrack.

Terrain: Forest; creek crossing.

Technical Level: Medium; some roots and ruts.

Exertion Level: Moderate; some climbing.

Highlights: An epic section of trail leading down to a creek before ascending back up. This trail connects Englesman and Eucalyptus Loops.

6G. Eucalyptus Loop Trail

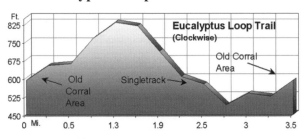

Distance: 3.5 miles.

Elevation: 490/830 ft.

Trail Surface: 29% singletrack; 71% fire road.

Terrain: Coastal grasslands; sparse forest; eucalyptus grove.

Technical Level: Medium.

Exertion Level: Moderate/Strenuous.

Highlights: This loop trail has some of the best panoramic ocean views in Wilder Ranch. Also connects with Chinquapin and the Gray Whale section.

Summer riding in Wilder Ranch on the Eucalyptus Loop Trail.

6H. Twin Oaks Trail

Distance: 1 mile.

Elevation: 390/615 ft.

Trail Surface: 100% singletrack.

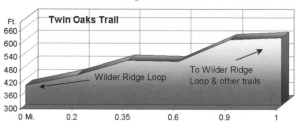

Terrain: Rolling grasslands with forested canyons.

Technical level: Medium.

Exertion Level: Moderate/Strenuous riding uphill.

Highlights: Rad singletrack section off of Wilder Ridge, that is being re-routed up and out of the swale at the time of press.

6I. Bobcat Trail

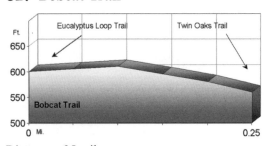

Distance: .25 miles.

Elevation: 560/610 ft.

Trail Surface: 100% singletrack.

Terrain: Sparse forest.

Technical Level: Medium.

Exertion Level: Easy.

Highlights: Groovy singletrack connecting Eucalyptus Loop to Twin Oaks.

6J. Wilder Ridge Loop Trail (in 3 sections)

"Fire Road Section"

Distance: 3 miles.

Elevation: 26/620 ft.

Trail Surface: 100% fire road.

Terrain: Coastal grasslands; sparse forest; ridges.

Technical Level: Easy/Medium.

Looking out at Wilder Beach from Wilder Ridge Fire Road.

Exertion Level: Moderate; one very strenuous but short section.

Highlights: This popular ride in the center of Wilder Ranch has a great viewpoint and access to other trails.

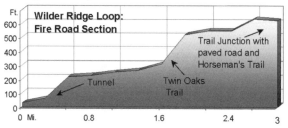

"Horseman's Trail"

Distance: 1.4 miles.

Elevation: 200/610 ft.

Trail Surface: 100% singletrack.

Terrain: Coastal grasslands; sparse forest; ridges.

Technical Level: Difficult; steep sections with ruts.

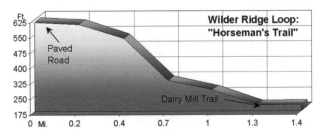

Exertion Level: Moderate riding downhill;
Very Strenuous riding uphill.

Highlights: Bomber Descent! Ruts, rocks, and steeps!

"Dairy Mill Trail" ("Old Dairy Trail")

Distance: 2.25 miles.

Elevation: 200/300 ft.

Tread: 100% singletrack.

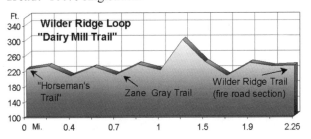

Trail Surface: Coastal grasslands; forest; creeks.

Technical Level: Moderate.

Exertion Level: Medium.

Highlights: Very fun winding section of singletrack!

6K. Zane Gray Trail

Distance: 1 mile.

Elevation: 200/300 ft.

Tread: 100% singletrack.

Trail Surface: Coastal grasslands; forest; small creek.

Technical Level: Difficult; some maneuvering required.

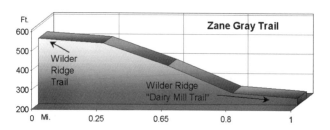

Exertion Level: Strenuous riding uphill.

Highlights: This epic trail is smooth at first with awesome views, then rutted and sometimes rocky.

6L. Cowboy Loop Trail

Distance: 1.9 miles.

Elevation: 55/255 ft.

Trail Surface: 100% singletrack; very rough in places.

Terrain: Coastal grasslands; forest; creek crossings.

Technical Level: Medium; Difficult in some sections.

Exertion Level: Moderate.

Highlights: This could be a great trail if more bikers rode it; however it is deteriorating and rutted with lots of deep hoof prints.

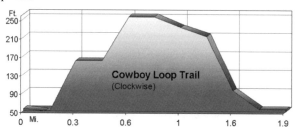

6M. Chinquapin Trail

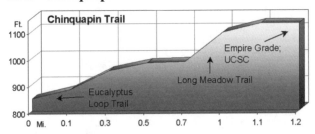

Distance: 1.2 miles.

Elevation: 850/1125 ft.

Trail Surface: 100% dirt road & doubletrack.

Terrain: Meadows; sparse forest.

Technical Level: Easy.

Exertion Level: Moderate; steady climbing.

Highlights: Connecting Wilder and Gray Whale Ranches with UCSC, this is a steady dirt road.

6N. Long Meadow Trail

Distance: 2.3 miles.

Elevation: 500/980 ft.

Trail Surface: 100% narrow fire road.

Terrain: Meadows; forested canyons.

Technical Level: Easy/medium.

Exertion Level: Moderate; steady climbing.

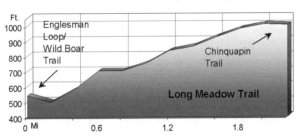

Highlights: This scenic trail has a steady climb heading toward UCSC and connects Wilder and Gray Whale Ranches.

60. Woodcutter's Trail

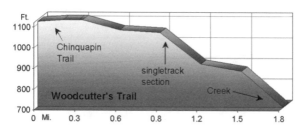

Distance: 1.8 miles one-way.

Elevation: 700/1100 ft.

Trail Surface: Fire road that has transformed into singletrack in some places.

Terrain: Forest; Creek.

Technical Level: Medium.

Exertion Level: Strenuous when climbing out.

Highlights: This trail would make a super fun loop if the nearby singletrack options were legal. But for now, it is to be ridden as an out & back ride.

A peaceful place to eat lunch devoid of the noise of civilization....
at the top of the Eucalyptus Loop Trail.

UCSC

Biker Jammin' up Chinquapin Road.

Centrally located between Wilder Ranch, Pogonip, and Henry Cowell, the University of California Santa Cruz is destined to be ridden. Although the Upper Campus area is jam-packed with sweet trails, most of them are currently closed to bikes. There are several nature reserves scattered throughout the area, in which hiking is the only permitted use on these once legally ridden trails. The residing rule states that mountain bikes are only allowed on designated dirt roads. However, the advocacy group, Mountain Bikers of Santa Cruz, is working hard to change policy and help open more trails on campus.

For now, Chinquapin Road is one of the most utilized "trails" in the upper campus. As this dirt road cuts through the length of the upper campus on its way to Wilder Ranch, it passes many of the other roads and trails in the area. The upper campus is open for riding from 5 am through 8 pm.

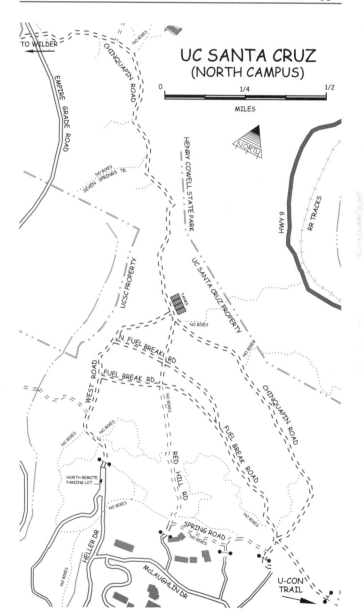

UC SANTA CRUZ
(NORTH CAMPUS)

0   1/4   1/2

MILES

NORTH

TO WILDER

CHINQUAPIN ROAD

EMPIRE GRADE ROAD

NO BIKES

SEVEN SPRINGS TR.

NO BIKES

HENRY COWELL STATE PARK

UC SANTA CRUZ PROPERTY

HWY 9

RR TRACKS

UCSC PROPERTY

TANKS

NO BIKES

NO BIKES

N. FUEL BREAK RD

FUEL BREAK RD.

WEST ROAD

CHINQUAPIN ROAD

NO BIKES

NO BIKES

NO BIKES

FUEL BREAK ROAD

NORTH REMOTE PARKING LOT

RED HILL RD

NO BIKES

NO BIKES

SPRING ROAD

NO BIKES

NO BIKES

HELLER DR

NO BIKES

McLAUGHLIN DR

U-CON TRAIL

Ride 7
North Campus Loop

Launching a little air in UCSC.

Location: University of California, Santa Cruz.

Distance: 3.1 miles minimum - on the most basic and direct loop. Many more miles are possible.

Elevation: 810/1035 ft.

Trail Surface: 100% fire roads.

Type of Ride: Loop.

Terrain: Shady forest.

Technical Level: Easy.

Exertion Level: Moderate.

Highlights: This network of trails provides good riding close to town. You can explore around, hit some jumps in the freestyle/bmx area, or just grind out a great cardio session.

Options: Explore!

Note: Beware; all the singletrack in the area is currently closed

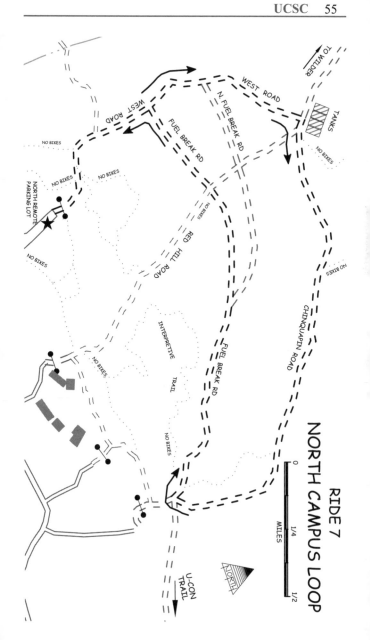

RIDE 7
NORTH CAMPUS LOOP

NORTH

0   1/4   1/2
MILES

TO WILDER

WEST   ROAD

TANKS

WEST ROAD

N. FUEL BREAK RD

NO BIKES

FUEL BREAK RD

NO BIKES

NORTH REMOTE PARKING LOT

NO BIKES

NO BIKES

NO BIKES

NO BIKES

NO BIKES

RED HILL ROAD

FUEL BREAK RD

CHINQUAPIN ROAD

NO BIKES

INTERPRETIVE

TRAIL

NO BIKES

NO BIKES

U-CON TRAIL

to bikers for preservation purposes. As insanely painful as it is, you are encouraged to ride only the legal fire roads.

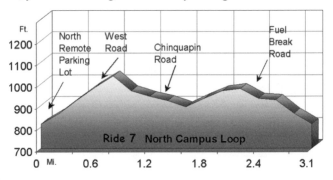

Directions/Access: Take Mission Street (Highway 1) north and turn right on Bay Dr. Just before the campus, turn left onto Empire Grade. Next, go right on Heller Street and take this all the way up to the North Remote Parking Lot. On weekends it is free to park here. Otherwise, you will need a parking pass. Many people will park off campus to avoid the hassle of parking here while school is in session. Also, refer to ride 9 for other parking options.

Mileage Guide	
0.0	In the North Remote Parking Lot, ride to the north end and go left on the fire road, West Rd. You will immediately pass by the gate labeled "UCSC Upper Campus."
.40	Ride past Fuel Break Road.
.50	Now you'll cruise by North Fuel Break Road.
.85	At the open area near the four large tanks, go right onto Chinquapin Road.
1.8	Turn right on Fuel Break Road.
2.3	At the split, stay to the left on Fuel Break Road. Soon you'll also pass by Red Hill Road.
2.7	Turn left on West Road to bomb back down.
3.1	Back at the parking lot.

Ride 8
Cowell-Wilder Regional Trail

The Cowell-Wilder Regional Trail.

Location: 2.5 miles out of Santa Cruz on Highway 9.
Distance: 8 miles. (Longer rides are possible; see Options).
Elevation: 300/1130 ft.
Trail Surface: 34% singletrack; 66% dirt & fire road.
Type of Ride: Out & Back; or Loop with UCSC trails.
Terrain: Forest, redwood groves, open grassland.
Technical Level: Medium.
Exertion Level: Moderate; gradual climbing.
Highlights: Linking Henry Cowell, Pogonip, and UCSC to

Wilder Ranch; this ride rates high on the fun factor! Some of the smoothest singletrack sections in the county! Scenic fire roads, berms, jumps, and lots of options!

Options: Although this ride is described as an out & back, most people create their own specialized loop rides using other trails in UCSC, Henry Cowell, or by crossing Empire Grade Road into Wilder Ranch. (See map). Pioneer-types will have fun exploring the area!

Note: Even though this ride passes several tempting single-track trails, just remember that only the dirt roads are open for biking on UCSC property at this time. The fact that some of these trails are closed is worth mourning over. Pray that the singletrack opens some day, because it would make for some incredible loop additions to this ride.

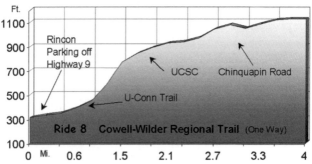

Directions/Access: From the intersection of Highways 17 and 1, go about 1 mile north on Highway 1. At the stop light at River Street, go right. This will turn into Highway 9. Take this for about 2.5 miles and park at the wide Rincon Trail pullout on the right. There is a gate with a dirt road leading across the train tracks. The trail is on the right just before the tracks.

Mileage Guide	
0.0	From the Rincon Turnout, ride past the gate and take the trail on the right. It's signed "Rincon Connector Trail" part of the "Cowell-Wilder Regional Trail."
.10	Cross Highway 9 and continue up the trail.

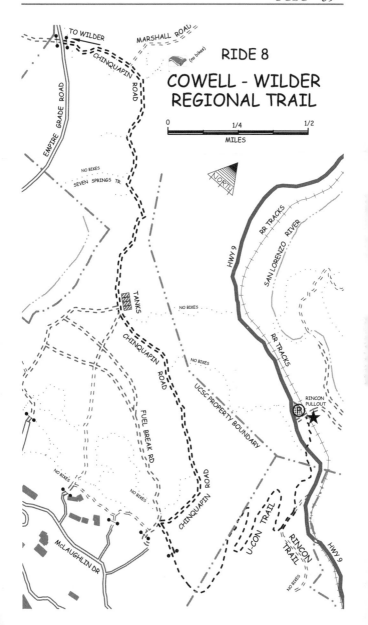

TO WILDER

MARSHALL ROAD

(no bikes)

CHINQUAPIN ROAD

EMPIRE GRADE ROAD

RIDE 8
COWELL - WILDER REGIONAL TRAIL

0   1/4   1/2

MILES

NORTH

NO BIKES

SEVEN SPRINGS TR.

RR TRACKS

SAN LORENZO RIVER

HWY 9

TANKS

NO BIKES

CHINQUAPIN ROAD

NO BIKES

RR TRACKS

FUEL BREAK RD

UCSC PROPERTY BOUNDARY

RINCON PULLOUT

★

NO BIKES

NO BIKES

CHINQUAPIN ROAD

NO BIKES

U-CON TRAIL

RINCON TRAIL

McLAUGHLIN DR

HWY 9

NO BIKES

.60	Merge right onto the service road signed "Rincon Trail." An information panel is just ahead.
.80	Turn right onto U-Con Trail at the sign, and enjoy this smooth singletrack on your way up to UCSC.
1.6	The UCSC information panel is at the top. Just ahead, veer right onto Fuel Break Road.
1.8	Pass around the gate.
1.9	Turn right on Chinquapin Road. Big air junkies can check out the BMX area ahead.
2.4	Ignore "Lock-em-Ups", an old horse trail steeply descending back to Highway 9, at the turn in the trail.
2.8	Tank area. On the right is another steep trail known as "Dead Camper Trail" (no bikes allowed). To the left, Red Hill and West Roads can be ridden. Go straight to continue on Chinquapin Road. The berms and jumps on the banks of this next section attest to the number of bikers who ride this road.
3.0	You will pass a series of nature reserve trails spurring off of Chinquapin Road over the next mile. Unfortunately, these are all closed to bike traffic.
4.0	Gate at Empire Grade Road. At this point, you may cross the road into Wilder/Gray Whale Ranch or turn around to ride back.
8.0	If you chose this ride as an Out & Back, you'll be back to the Rincon pullout now.

Riding in UCSC.

The tanks at the conjunction of Chinquapin Road, Red Hill Road,
West Road, and Dead Camper Trail.

Ride 9
Arroyo Seco-UCSC-Wilder Loop

Location: Santa Cruz; near Swift Street.

Distance: 14 miles.

Elevation: 30/1130 ft.

Trail Surface: 22% singletrack; 48% fire & dirt roads; 21% paved bike path; 9% paved road.

Type of Ride: Loop.

Terrain: Forest; grasslands; creeks; ocean views; UCSC.

Technical Level: Medium.

Exertion Level: Strenuous; a good amount of climbing.

Highlights: This excellent loop ride from town heads up Arroyo Seco canyon, through UCSC, down Gray Whale and Wilder Ranch, and back along the County Bike Path. The Arroyo Seco section is an enjoyable alternative to riding up Bay Street for access to the UCSC trails.

Options: There are many ways to tweak this ride to fit your wildest desires. With a variety of trails in UCSC, Gray Whale and Wilder, you have ample ability to pick and choose trails. The described ride is only one suggestion, as well as the most direct.

Note: Just another reminder that bikes are not allowed on the UCSC Nature Preserve trails, unless changes in policy occur.

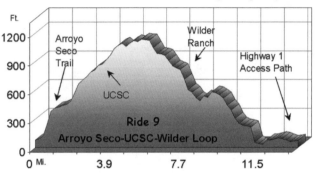

Directions/Access: Take Mission St (Highway 1) north and turn right on Swift St. Veer left as the road soon turns into Grand View St. Go about 100 yards after the stop sign. Park near the Santa Cruz Mission Garden Park on the right. The trail starts in between the chain link fence and stucco wall to the right of the small park.

Mileage Guide	
0.0	Take the trail between the chain link fence and stucco wall to the right of the park. At first it is a gravel path, but immediately turns into a dirt trail.
.10	Cross the bridge over creek and follow the singletrack into the Eucalyptus grove.
.20	After another bridge, the trail heads left and becomes a wider path now.
.50	Split. Go left up the gradual incline.
.80	As the trail becomes paved, keep going straight.
1.0	Exit the forest into the park area.
1.1	Go right on Meder Street and ride to Bay Street.

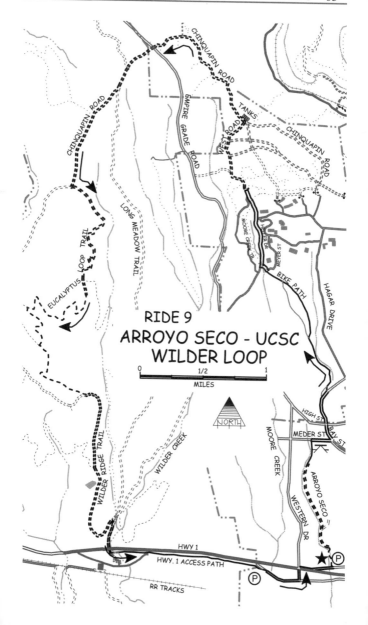

RIDE 9
ARROYO SECO - UCSC
WILDER LOOP

1.3	Turn left on Bay Street and ride up the bike lane.
1.5	Cross High Street and ride into UCSC. Stay on the same road until you reach the top of the hill.
1.8	At the 1st intersection as the road flattens, turn left toward the "Farm" area. Just after this turn, spot the green sign and take the paved bike path on your right.
2.8	Bike Path ends. Pass the stop sign and go straight on Meyer Street.
3.0	Major Intersection. Across the street, there is a great singletrack that leads up to the upper campus trails. However, it has become part of the UCSC Nature Reserve and is officially off limits to bikes. This may change in the future, hopefully, with the efforts of MBOSC. Until more trails are opened, go right on Heller Street. (There is a little trail on the right side of the road for avoiding the traffic).
3.4	At the intersection, with a parking structure on the right, continue straight ahead on Heller Street.
3.6	Ride straight through the parking area.
3.7	At the end of the parking area, veer left on the dirt road, West Road. Ride around the gate labeled "UCSC Upper Campus" and continue up.
4.1	Pedal past Fuel Break and North Fuel Break Roads.
4.5	When you come to the open space at the tanks, go left on Chinquapin. You will ride by many closed trails in this next section.
5.7	Gate. Cross Empire Grade and ride past the gate into Wilder/Gray Whale Ranch.
6.0	Continue on Chinquapin and pass Woodcutter Trail off to the right..
6.2	Roll on by Long Meadow Trail.
7.1	Head left on the Eucalyptus Loop at the end of Chinquapin.
8.2	After you pass Old Cabin Trail, the road will soon become singletrack as you descend into the forest.

*After climbing through UCSC, a rider enjoys
descending the trails in Wilder Ranch.*

9.2	Split. Go left on Bobcat Trail, which will soon merge into Twin Oaks Trail. Keep heading downhill!
10.1	Veer left onto Wilder Ridge Trail (fire road).
11.7	At the bottom, turn right and head for the tunnel.
11.8	Just after passing under the tunnel, turn left on the bike path that parallels Highway 1 South.
12.3	Check out the BMX area on the left (if it hasn't been destroyed by officials)!
13.2	When you reach the dirt parking area, keep riding straight ahead on Shaffer Drive.
13.5	Turn left on Western Drive and cross Highway 1. Then take an immediate right on Grand View Drive (closed to cars on this side).
13.9	Return to the park where you started.

Rides 10 A-E
UCSC Trail Guide

10A. Chinquapin Road (UCSC section)

Distance: 2.1 miles.

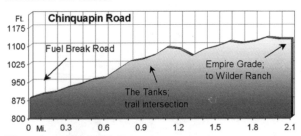

Elevation: 880/1130 ft.

Trail Surface: 100% dirt road.

Terrain: Forest; meadows.

Technical Level: Easy.

Exertion Level: Moderate.

Highlights: Providing access to many other trails in the area, this widely used road is the main link between Pogonip and Wilder Ranch.

10B. Fuel Break Road

Distance: 1 mile.
Elevation: 830/958 ft.

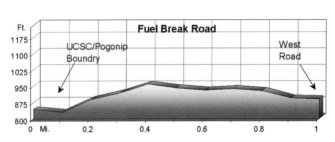

Trail Surface: 100% dirt road.

Terrain: Forest.

Technical Level: Easy.

Exertion Level: Moderate; fairly steep climbs in the beginning.

Highlights: Fuel Break is another widely used road that cuts through the upper campus and meets up with Chinquapin Road near Pogonip.

10C. North Fuel Break Road

Distance: .4 miles.

Elevation: 925/980 ft.

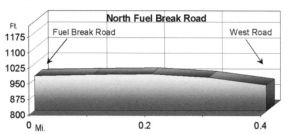

Trail Surface: 100% dirt road.

Terrain: Forest, chaparral.

Technical Level: Easy.

Exertion Level: Moderate.

Highlights: A short segment, this road is an offshoot of Fuel Break Road.

10D. West Road

Distance: .8 miles.

Elevation: 820/1040 ft.

Trail Surface: 100% dirt road.

Terrain: Forest, chaparral.

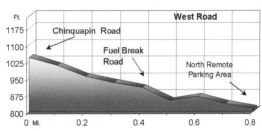

Technical Level: Easy.

Exertion Level: Moderate/ Strenuous; a steep climb.

Highlights: This road directly links the campus parking area to Chinquapin and Fuel Break Roads.

10E. Red Hill Road

Distance: .3 miles.

Elevation: 960/1050 ft.

Trail Surface: 100% dirt road.

Terrain: Forest.

Technical Level: Easy.

Exertion Level: Moderate.

Highlights: Paralleling West Road, Red Hill Road also bisects North Fuel Break and Fuel Break Roads. The lower section of this road near the campus buildings is off limits to bikes, however.

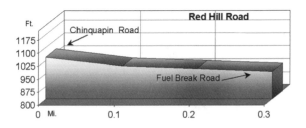

Pogonip Park

Smooth winding singletrack on the U-Con Trail.

Pogonip is a City of Santa Cruz Greenbelt Park with a scenic 640-acre expanse of open meadows, woodlands, and creeks. While mountain bike trails are limited in number, there is one fabulous route open. Providing non-stop biking access from Henry Cowell to UCSC, this ridable section includes Rincon Connector Trail, Rincon Road, and the U-Con Trail.

The park is open from sunrise to 7 pm in the summer and until 4 pm in the winter. Located between UCSC and highway 9, the mountain bike parking is at the Rincon Pullout about 2.5 miles north of Santa Cruz.

Ride 11
The U-Con Trail
(with Rincon Connector Trail)

Sights from Pogonip.

Location: 2.5 miles north of Santa Cruz on Highway 9.

Distance: 3.2 miles roundtrip.

Elevation: 310/840 ft.

Trail Surface: 85% singletrack; 15% narrow fire road.

Terrain: Redwood forest.

Type of Ride: Out & Back.

Technical Difficulty: Easy/Medium.

Exertion Level: Easy/Moderate; due to its short length.

Highlights: For a quick fix, this is a great short ride. Some of the most smooth-to-the-groove singletrack around!

Options: For a longer ride, see Ride 8.

Note: This is the only permitted ride in Pogonip.

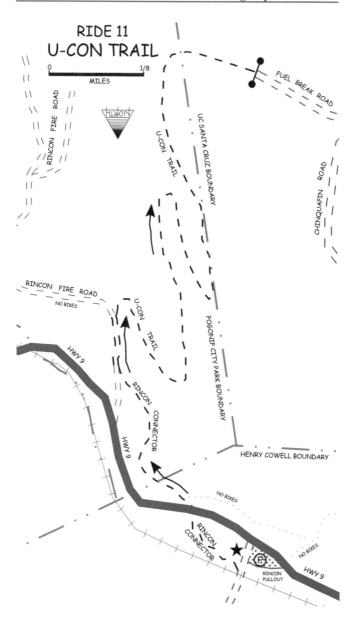

RIDE 11
U-CON TRAIL

0   MILES   1/8

NORTH

FUEL BREAK ROAD

RINCON FIRE ROAD

U-CON TRAIL

UC SANTA CRUZ BOUNDARY

CHINQUAPIN ROAD

RINCON FIRE ROAD

NO BIKES

U-CON TRAIL

POGONIP CITY PARK BOUNDARY

HWY 9

RINCON CONNECTOR

HENRY COWELL BOUNDARY

NO BIKES

HWY 9

RINCON CONNECTOR

NO BIKES

HWY 9

RINCON PULLOUT

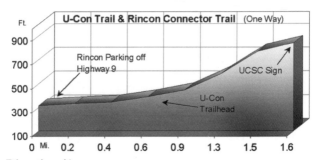

Directions/Access:

From the intersection of Highways 17 and 1, go about 1 mile north on Highway 1. At the stop light at River Street, go right. This will turn into Highway 9. Take this for about 2.5 miles and park at the wide "Rincon Parking" pullout on the right. There is a gate there with a dirt road leading across the train tracks. The trail is on the right before the tracks.

Mileage Guide	
0.0	From the Rincon Turnout, ride down past the gate and take the trail on the right (before you come to the railroad tracks). It's signed "Rincon Connector Trail."
.10	Cross Highway 9.
.60	Merge right onto the service road signed "Rincon Trail."
.80	Turn right onto U-Con Trail at the sign.
1.6	At the top is a UCSC information panel. Time to turn around for some groovin' downhill fun!
3.2	Back at parking lot.

Riders mountain biking through Pogonip on the U-Con Trail.

Henry Cowell Redwoods State Park

Riding down Ridge Fire Road.

If you enjoy big trees, Henry Cowell is the place to bike. The main park area contains 1,750 acres of large old-growth redwoods, while the northern Fall Creek area includes 2,390 acres. Within this massive congregation of trees is a redwood that is 285 feet tall and about 16 feet wide. Having sprouted during the era of the Roman Empire, some of these trees are 1400 to 1800 years old. In addition to redwood groves, the park is filled with douglas fir, madrone, oak, and some ponderosa pine.

With 20 miles of trails, the park is filled with hikers, horseback riders, and bikers. While the singletrack trails are closed to mountain bikes, cycling is permitted on Pipeline Road, Rincon Fire Road, Ridge Fire Road, and Powder Mill Fire Road.

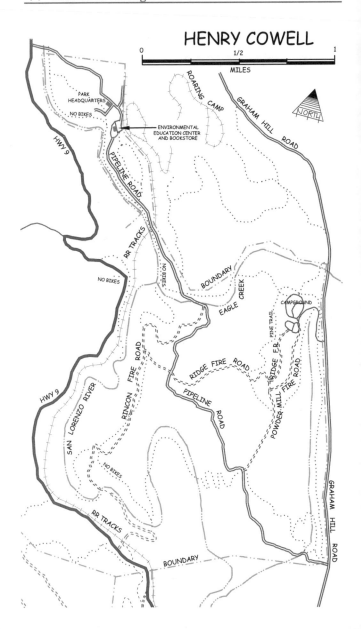

HENRY COWELL

0   1/2   1
MILES

NORTH

PARK
HEADQUARTERS
NO BIKES

ROARING CAMP

GRAHAM HILL ROAD

ENVIRONMENTAL
EDUCATION CENTER
AND BOOKSTORE

HWY 9

PIPELINE ROAD

RR TRACKS

NO BIKES

NO BIKES

BOUNDARY

EAGLE CREEK

CAMPGROUND

PINE TRAIL

RINCON FIRE ROAD

RIDGE FIRE ROAD

RIDGE F.R.

POWDER MILL FIRE ROAD

PIPELINE ROAD

HWY 9

SAN LORENZO RIVER

NO BIKES

RR TRACKS

BOUNDARY

GRAHAM HILL ROAD

The park has some scenic picnic areas above the San Lorenzo River, a campground, nature center, and a bookstore. There are no bridges for biking across the San Lorenzo River.

The main park entrance is located near Felton on Highway 9. The Rincon Fire Road parking lot is on the south side of the park off Highway 9 about three miles south of the main entrance. The Powder Mill trailhead and parking lot is off Graham Hill Road just north of Sims Road in Santa Cruz.

Ride 12
Henry Cowell Loop

The observation deck, a popular rest stop, has great mountain and ocean views, as well as a drinking fountain.

Location: 6 miles north of Santa Cruz off highway 9.

Distance: 5.6 - 8.3 miles; depending on options chosen.

Elevation: 240/740 ft.

Trail Surface: 58% narrow fire road; 42% paved fire road.

Type of Ride: Loop with an optional out & back section.

Terrain: Redwood groves; San Lorenzo River.

Technical Level: Moderate; one deep sandy area. The ride rates a bit more difficult if riding the optional section down to the river on Rincon Fire Road. (This involves a steeper section with more rocks and roots).

Exertion Level: Strenuous; some steep sections.

Highlights: Providing a wonderful workout on smooth fire roads, this ride has some truly great scenery and a beautiful access to the river.

Options: You can ride an out & back section on Rincon Fire Road to the river; see the Mileage Guide below for details.

Note: There is no bridge over the river, but it can be crossed at low flows in the summer. Use caution!

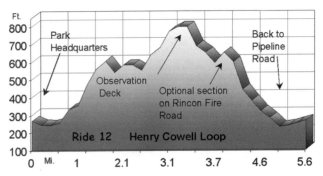

Directions/Access: Take Highway 1 into Santa Cruz. At the stop light at River Street in Santa Cruz, go right onto Highway 9. About 6 miles later, you'll see the main entrance to Henry Cowell on the right. Parking is $3. To avoid this fee, park in the pullout on Highway 9 just before the entrance. The main parking and visitor center is about .6 miles from the entrance.

Mileage Guide	
0.0	From the main parking lot near the visitor center, take one of the paved trails down to Pipeline Road; (located on either the lefthand or righthand sides of the visitor center area).
.10	Pipeline Road. At the main sign, go straight. (The creek will be on your right).

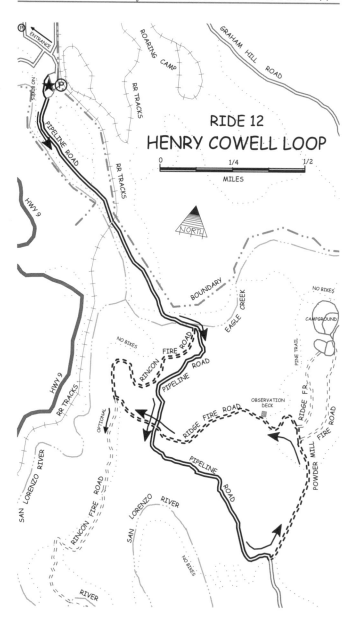

ENTRANCE

NO BIKES

PIPELINE ROAD

ROARING CAMP

RR TRACKS

GRAHAM HILL ROAD

RR TRACKS

RIDE 12
HENRY COWELL LOOP

0   1/4   1/2
MILES

NORTH

HWY 9

BOUNDARY

EAGLE CREEK

NO BIKES

CAMPGROUND

PINE TRAIL

NO BIKES

RINCON FIRE ROAD

PIPELINE ROAD

RIDGE FIRE ROAD

OBSERVATION DECK

RIDGE F.R.

POWDER MILL FIRE ROAD

HWY 9

RR TRACKS

OPTIONAL

SAN LORENZO RIVER

RINCON FIRE ROAD

PIPELINE ROAD

SAN LORENZO RIVER

NO BIKES

RIVER

1.1	Keep cranking up the steep hill past Rincon Fire Road.
1.6	Bike beyond the Ridge Fire Road turnoff.
1.7	Don't miss the nice viewpoint on the right!
2.4	Go left at the picnic area onto Powder Mill Fire Road.
2.9	Go straight, ignoring the road on the right that heads to the campground.
3.0	At Ridge Road, go left up to the observation deck.
3.2	Observation Deck. Enjoy the great panoramic views! If it's clear, you can see the ocean, Monterey, and several forested hills leading up to Skyline. There is also an information panel, drinking fountain, and a picnic area. To continue on the fire road, stay to the left and head down the backside. The next .4 miles has water-bar drop-offs and may be very sandy; at least its downhill!
3.8	Cross Pipeline Road and keep going on Ridge Fire Rd.
4.0	Rincon Fire Road. To add another 2.7 miles, go left and ride an out & back section down to the river (or a shorter section to the Cathedral Redwoods). For more information on this section see the Ride 13 Mileage Guide (Miles 1.3-2.7). Otherwise, go right to finish the loop.
4.2	Keep right. You'll pass the River Trail on the left.
4.5	Go Left on Pipeline Road.
5.6	That's all folks; you should be back at the main parking area.

Looking over the Henry Cowell campground toward the ocean from the observation deck.

Ride 13
Redwoods to Coast Ride

Heading toward the San Lorenzo River on Rincon Fire Road.

Location: Off Graham Hill Rd, 3 miles from Santa Cruz.

Distance: 15.6 miles one-way; 31.2+ miles as a loop.

Elevation: 50/1130 ft.

Trail Surface: 30% singletrack; 70% dirt & fire road.

Type of Ride: One-Way shuttle; or an Loop/Out & Back for the hardcore.

Terrain: Redwoods; San Lorenzo River; grasslands; coastal cliffs; lots of great views!

Technical Level: Difficult; some rutted, rocky, and sandy areas.

Exertion Level: Strenuous as a one-way; Very Strenuous when riding as a loop.

Highlights: An epic ride! Combining Henry Cowell, Pogonip, UCSC, and Wilder Ranch, it takes you all the way from the redwoods of Felton to crashing surf on the cliffs. During this ride you will enjoy the huge spectrum of terrain that Santa

Cruz has to offer.

Options: There are many other trails to explore on the way down, particularly in Wilder Ranch. If you are in a super gonzo mood, you can ride it as a loop/out & back.

Note: This ride has one of the biggest river crossings in Santa Cruz and is not recommended in the winter due to high flow. The river should be avoided between November and April in most years. Please use sound judgment when crossing.

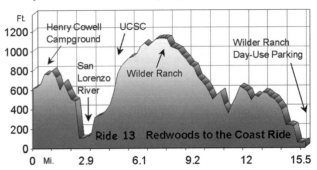

Directions/Access: The shuttle drop-off at Wilder Ranch involves driving a couple miles north of Santa Cruz on Highway 1, and leaving a car in the state park day-use parking ($5). You may also park in the dirt pullout to the left off Highway 1 just before the main entrance.

The ride begins in Henry Cowell. From Ocean St in Santa Cruz (off of Highway 1, by the intersection of Highway 17), go right onto Graham Hill Road. After about 3 miles, turn left into Henry Cowell Park/Campground and drive to the entrance booth. Parking is $3 when staffed. You can park near the booth or .1 mile further up on the left by the Powder Mill trailhead.

Mileage Guide	
0.0	From the Powder Mill Trailhead, ride around the gate onto the fire road.
.40	At the signed intersection, go right onto Ridge Fire Road. You will soon come to another split; go left.

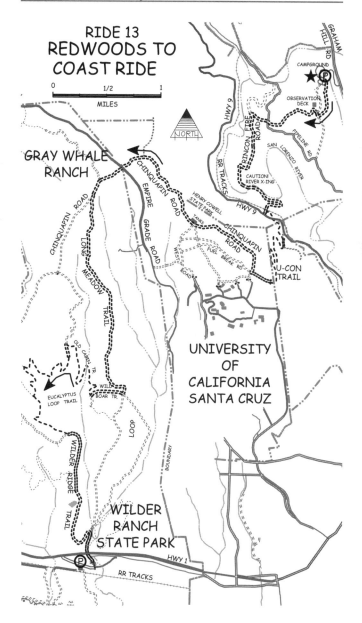

RIDE 13
REDWOODS TO COAST RIDE

0   1/2   1
MILES

NORTH

GRAY WHALE RANCH

CHINQUAPIN ROAD

EMPIRE GRADE ROAD

CHINQUAPIN ROAD

LONG MEADOW TRAIL

OLD CABIN TR.

WILD BOAR TR.

EUCALYPTUS LOOP TRAIL

WILDER RIDGE TRAIL

WILDER LOOP

BOUNDARY

WILDER RANCH STATE PARK

UNIVERSITY OF CALIFORNIA SANTA CRUZ

GRAHAM HILL RD

CAMPGROUND

OBSERVATION DECK

PIPELINE RD

SAN LORENZO RIVER

HWY 9

RINCON FIRE ROAD

RR TRACKS

CAUTION! RIVER X-ING

HENRY COWELL STATE PARK

TANKS

CHINQUAPIN ROAD

FUEL BREAK RD.

WEST ROAD

U-CON TRAIL

HWY 1

RR TRACKS

.60	Observation Deck with panoramic views! Continuing on the fire road, stay to the left and head down the backside. The next .4-mile section is one big sand trap in the summer, with many water-bar drop offs.
1.1	Cross Pipeline Road and keep going on Ridge Fire Rd.
1.3	Go left on Rincon Fire Road. Soon you will ride through the "Cathedral Redwoods."
1.8	This can be somewhat confusing; a trail crosses diagonally here. Go straight (toward the right).
2.2	Keep left (straight) and pass the Diversion Dam trail. The road will now have progressively more roots, rocks, and trees; as well as some very steep sections.
2.7	San Lorenzo River. After crossing, spot the trail on the other side. Stay straight on the path as it leads into the fire road toward the left. (Ignore the Diversion Dam trail on right). The road will be flat at first before weaving its way up the cliff to the train tracks.
3.5	Are you ready for some singletrack yet?! Cross the tracks and take Rincon Connector Trail on the left.
3.6	Cross Highway 9 and continue on the trail.
4.1	Merge onto the service road signed "Rincon Trail," heading to the right.
4.3	Turn right onto U-Con Trail at the sign.
5.1	Soon after the UCSC information panel at the top, you will merge right onto Fuel Break Road.
5.4	Turn right on Chinquapin Road. Continue on the main road for a couple miles passing all the spur trails and intersections.
7.5	Twin Gates at Empire Grade Road. Cross over into Wilder Ranch and continue on Chinquapin Road.
7.8	Ignoring Woodcutter Trail, stay to the left.
8.0	Turn left onto Long Meadow Trail.
10.2	Stay to the right (toward the ocean) on the main trail as you pass by a spur trail near the old quarry ruins.

10.3	Major Intersection! All directions will eventually lead down to the same spot. For more singletrack, we recommend going right on Wild Boar trail.
10.6	Turn right onto Old Cabin Trail and enjoy a fun singletrack section.
11.6	Turn left onto Eucalyptus Loop Trail; this will soon become another great singletrack segment.
12.6	After crossing the creek, take Bobcat trail (singletrack) on the left.
12.9	The trail runs into Twin Oaks Trail; keep bombing down!
13.6	Next, the trail merges onto Wilder Ridge Loop Trail. Keep to the left and take this all the way down.
15.1	Go right when you reach the turn-off at the bottom, and head past the information panel toward the tunnel.
15.4	After crossing under the tunnel, walk your bikes through the Cultural Preserve. When you come to the main paved access road, go right and ride up toward the bathrooms and parking lot.
15.6	Wilder Ranch day-use parking area.

Commencing in thick forest, the "Redwoods to Coast Ride"
ends with fantastic ocean views.

Rides 14 A-E
Henry Cowell Trail Guide

14A. Rincon Connector Trail

Distance: .6 miles.

Elevation: 305/390 ft.

Trail Surface: 100% singletrack.

Terrain: Forest; Highway 9 crossing.

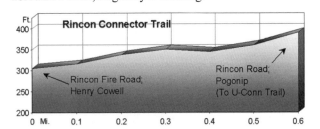

Technical Level: Easy/Moderate.

Exertion Level: Mild.

Highlights: This smooth and groovy trail connects Rincon Road in Henry Cowell to Pogonip, UCSC, and Wilder Ranch. (This trail is partially located in Pogonip).

14B. Rincon Fire Road

Distance: 2.7 miles.

Elevation: 100/670 ft.

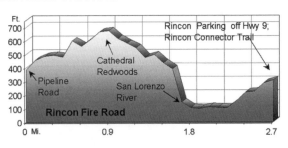

Trail Surface: 100% narrow fire road; "almost" singletrack.

Terrain: Redwood groves; San Lorenzo River crossing.

Technical Level: Medium; the steep rutted section descending to the river can rate more difficult, however.

Exertion Level: Moderate/Strenuous.

Highlights: Connecting Pipeline and Ridge Roads to the Rincon Parking area on highway 9, this road winds through the "Cathedral Redwoods" down to the river (usually not passable from Nov. to April) and back up to the Rincon Connector Trail.

14C. Ridge Fire Road

Distance: 1.1 miles.

Elevation: 570/800 ft.

Trail Surface: 100% fire road; narrow at times with some sand and drop offs.

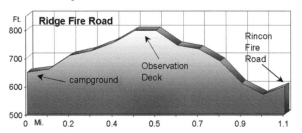

Terrain: Forest; observation deck with panoramic views.

Technical Level: Medium; the toughest section is on the sandy backside of the observation deck.

Exertion Level: Moderate.

Highlights: The 360-degree views make this trail well worth it. It connects with Pipeline, Powder Mill, and Rincon Roads.

14D. Powder Mill Fire Road

Distance: 1 mile.

Elevation: 555/690 ft.

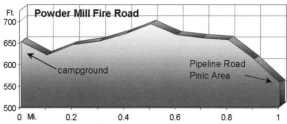

Trail Surface: 100% fire road.

Terrain: Dense forest; campground; picnic area.

Technical Level: Easy.

Exertion Level: Moderate.

Highlights: Cruising from the campground to the Pipeline Road picnic area, this fire road also connects with Ridge Fire Road near the observation deck.

14E. Pipeline Road

Distance: 3 miles.

Elevation: 250/590 ft.

Trail Surface: 100% paved fire road.

Terrain: San Lorenzo River; redwoods; viewpoint.

Technical Level: Easy.

Exertion Level: Moderate/Strenuous; lots of hills. However, the first section near the the river is a flatter and easier ride.

Highlights: This trail bisects the park and provides access to many trails between Highway 9 and Graham Hill Road.

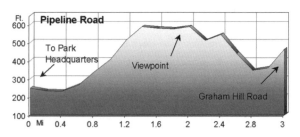

DeLaveaga Park

Airing over a big root on the Figure 8 Loop.

DeLaveaga is a perfect example of what makes Santa Cruz so awesome! Thanks to the immense generosity of Jose DeLaveaga in 1894, there's a big chunk of open space dedicated to nothing but recreation. A challenging golf course, a world class disc golf course, an archery course, athletic fields, playgrounds….and, of course, sweet singletrack! While many of the trails are somewhat short, there is plenty of exploration to be had. Rides for all skill levels will love DeLaveaga Park, whether you want a short family cruiser, a fast rollercoaster singletrack, or a freestyle and downhiller playground. DeLaveaga is part of the City of Santa Cruz Parks & Recreation Department. It is open for biking from 7 am to Sunset in the winter and from 7 am to 11 pm in the summer.

Ride 15
Top of The World Loop

Riding the Top of the World Trail.

Location: In Santa Cruz off of Branciforte Street.

Distance: At least 4.5 miles.

Elevation: 120/450 ft.

Trail Surface: 60% singletrack (much more is possible); 20% fire road; 20% paved road.

Type of Ride: Loop.

Terrain: Forest; disc golf; golf course; great views.

Technical Level: Medium; mostly smooth with some drop-offs and scattered roots.

Exertion Level: Moderate.

Highlights: Great short loop with panoramic ocean views at Top of the World. It's all about smooth fast sections, technical areas, berms and banks! In addition, there are spur trails with steep shoots throughout the ride to test willing egos.

Options: You can also ride this as an out & back. However, be aware of speedy descenders. Bring your frisbee discs!

Note: This loop involves a golf course crossing which can be very dangerous! Please do not interrupt the golfers' games; they might get mad and whack a ball at you. To avoid this crossing, either ride the trail as an out & back or ride up the main golf course road, Upper Park Road, from the beginning.

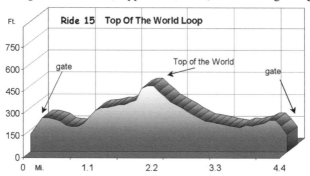

Directions/Access: From Highway 17 or 1, take "Ocean St./Beaches" exit. Get in the left-hand turn lane, and go left at the very first light on Plymouth Drive. Then you will take a quick right on Grant Street and follow the road down. When you reach Market Street, take a left and go under the freeway. After passing the first stop sign, look for the dirt parking lot on the right about 500 feet ahead. The ride starts at the gate on the far side of the pullout.

Mileage Guide	
0.0	Pedal around the gate and head up the fire road.
.10	On the left is a superb singletrack option. This trail will parallel and meet up with the fire road at the .75-mile mark on this Mileage Guide.

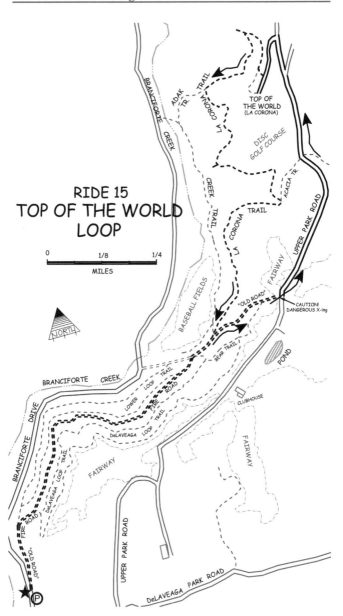

RIDE 15
TOP OF THE WORLD
LOOP

.20	The fire road will gradually flatten out and start to descend for a while.
.75	On the left, a trail merges with the fire road.
.80	Major intersection area! Up the hillside on the right, there is access to the upper trails (see Ride 16). On the left, another fire road descends to Branciforte Street. Just past this road on the left, is La Corona Trail, which leads to Top of the World. This option can be taken for an out & back ride. Otherwise, continue straight on the main fire road as it climbs to the golf course.
1.2	The fire road ends at the golf course. No biking is allowed on the golf course. However, if no golfers are around, you can carry your bike and head directly across the green (about 100 feet) to the paved golf course road. Please be cautious of flying golf balls and be courteous to golfers! After crossing, go left and ride up the road.
1.7	At the disc golf parking area, take the left-most road at the split.
1.9	At this next split, go left past either side of the gate. You'll pass a very steep singletrack shoot on the right. Keep riding up the ridge.
2.0	After the road flattens and widens, look for the unmarked singletrack dropping off on the right. At first, it heads back the direction you just came. (However, before taking this trail, ride up a little further to view all of Santa Cruz and Monterey Bay! This is Top of the World and disc golf hole #27).
2.2	At the intersection, make a sharp left turn. To the right is a steep trail that heads toward private property.
2.6	Park bench and viewpoint on the right. A couple steep and rough trails descend here. On the left, show-offs often tear down the steep shoots. Keep heading straight to continue on.
3.5	You are now back in the intersection area on the main fire road (see Mile .80). Rides may be extended by

	riding the upper trails on the left. To continue back to the entrance there are many options: 1. Take the main fire road down. 2. Take the other fire road (descending on the right) just a little way to the singletrack that will be on your left. This will take you back to the main fire road just above the gate and parking area. 3. Ride about a couple hundred feet on the main fire road (left) and take the singletrack on your right. This also will take you back to the gate and parking area.
4.4	Gate.

*Enjoying the ocean view near the disc golf launch pad
at Top of the World.*

Ride 16
Figure 8 Loop

Location: In Santa Cruz off of Branciforte Street.

Miles: 3.5 miles.

Elevation: 120/310 ft.

Trail Surface: 98% singletrack; 2% fire road.

Type of Ride: Loop.

Terrain: Forest; golf course; steep slopes; some big roots.

Technical Level: Medium; mostly smooth with occasional steeps, drop-offs and scattered roots.

Exertion Level: Moderate.

Cruisin' DeLaveaga Style!

Highlights: Maximizing the singletrack in DeLaveaga Park, this great short loop is fun for all riding abilities. Enjoy smooth fast sections with a few technical areas and plenty of playful features on this double loop ride.

Options: Ride in different directions. For a longer ride, combine with Ride 15 or any of the other DeLaveaga trails.

Note: The trails are unsigned and may be slightly confusing at first… good thing you have this guide!

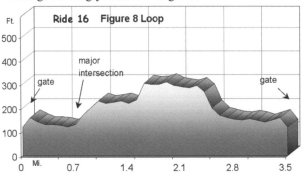

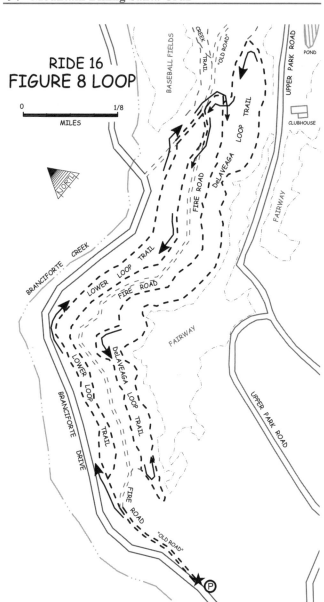

RIDE 16
FIGURE 8 LOOP

0   1/8

MILES

NORTH

BASEBALL FIELDS

CREEK TRAIL

"OLD ROAD"

UPPER PARK ROAD

POND

CLUBHOUSE

DeLAVEAGA LOOP TRAIL

FIRE ROAD

FAIRWAY

BRANCIFORTE CREEK

LOWER LOOP TRAIL

FIRE ROAD

FAIRWAY

UPPER PARK ROAD

BRANCIFORTE DRIVE

LOWER LOOP TRAIL

DeLAVEAGA LOOP TRAIL

FIRE ROAD

"OLD ROAD"

P

Directions/Access: See Ride 15.

Having fun in DeLaveaga.

Mileage Guide	
0.0	Pedal around the gate and ride up the fire road.
.10	Go left on the unmarked singletrack. Fun, fun, fun, and more fun is just ahead!
.20	Stay to left at the split.
.70	The trail ends as you reach the semi-paved fire road. Go right and ride up the road to the intersection.
.80	Main intersection. Veer a little to the right and ride toward the hillside bank in front of you. Take the trail which switchbacks its way up and eventually heads to the right (ignore the other trail that merges on the left).
1.3	Huge tree roots are blocking the route; either a mega bunny hop or a quick dismount is necessary.
1.6	Stay on the main trail as it curves around and parallels the golf course. Lots of rolly-polly action ahead!
2.4	Make a sharp left here! Otherwise, the trail to the right leads to an intersection higher up on the main fire road.
2.5	As you reach the switchbacks again, make a sharp right

	to head down
2.6	Back at the main intersection, turn left and ride on the main fire road for a couple hundred feet. Then take the sweet singletrack dropping off to the right.
3.2	Keep heading straight as the lower trail merges.
3.4	Once again you're at the main fire road. If you're ready to call it a day, turn right and head down to the gate.
3.5	Return to parking area.

A sunny oak-studded section of trail in DeLaveaga.

Forest of Nisene Marks State Park

Cruising one of the many singletrack trails in lower Nisene Marks.

With 10,000 acres of rugged terrain stretching from sea level to lush 3000-foot mountains, The Forest of Nisene Marks lives up to its association as a premier mountain biking destination. Although only some of the 30+ miles of smooth-as-silk 'trails' are legal for bikers; the fabulous viewpoints, redwood forest, perennial creeks, and tacky soil make mountain biking here a magnificent experience. A giant "thank you" goes out to the Marks family, who donated the land to the public in 1963.

"Lower Nisene," the area below the steel bridge, contains some great singletrack. Here, Aptos Creek Fire Road commences and scenically winds its way up through the entire length of the park. Beyond the steel bridge in "Upper Nisene," bikes are currently only allowed on the fire roads. At the time of press, the Nisene Marks General Plan, which concerns the status of trails, is being reviewed. If you would like to see more ridable singletrack, voice your opinions!

Besides biking, Nisene Marks offers many interesting side excursions as well. As you ride around, you'll encounter evidence of century-old logging operations, mill sites, and trestles throughout the park. Other interesting features include several impressive waterfalls, the Loma Prieta Earthquake Epicenter and the Advocate, a giant redwood with a 45-foot circumference. In addition, the park contains a backpacker camp and many picnic areas.

The main entrance is located 6 miles southeast of Santa Cruz off of Soquel Drive in Aptos. Day-use parking near the entrance booth on Aptos Creek Road costs a small fee when the booth is staffed.

Dropping a large root on Aptos Rancho Trail.

SANTA ROSALIA OVERLOOK

SOQUEL DEMONSTRATION FOREST

HIGHLAND WAY

BUZZARD LAGOON ROAD

PARK BOUNDARY

HINCKLEY CREEK

APTOS CREEK FIRE ROAD

SAND POINT OVERLOOK

HINCKLEY BASIN FIRE ROAD

BIG SLIDE

APTOS CREEK FIRE ROAD

APTOS CREEK TR.

APTOS CREEK

BRIDGE CREEK

PARK BOUNDARY

LOMA PRIETA GRADE

WEST RIDGE TRAIL

NISENE MARKS STATE PARK

0   1   2

MILES

STEEL BRIDGE

NORTH

LOWER NISENE TRAILS

APTOS CREEK RD.

SOQUEL DR

HWY 1

Ride 17
Aptos Rancho Trail

Location: Aptos; about 6 miles southeast of Santa Cruz.

Distance: 4 miles.

Elevation: 55/180 ft.

Trail Surface: 100% singletrack.

Type of Ride: Out & Back; many loop rides are possible.

Terrain: Redwood forest; creek crossing.

Technical Level: Medium; some short sections with random roots, ruts, drop-offs, and log obstacles that are more difficult.

Exertion Level: Easy/Moderate; many short fluctuations in elevation gain/loss.

Highlights: This sweet Nisene trail is a fast and groovy singletrack with enough jibs and root drops to make it interesting! As is typical of Nisene rides, you will encounter lush forest scenery along Aptos Creek which meanders through moss and fern covered cliffs visible below the trail.

Options: Loops are possible with Aptos Creek Fire Road or Terrace Trail. Add Ride 18 or Split Stuff to lengthen the ride.

Note: Creek crossings can be sketchy at high flows (Dec.-March). Look for natural rock crossings at lower flows. Also, be cautious of hikers and joggers who often use this trail.

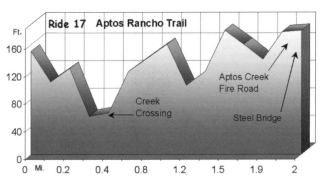

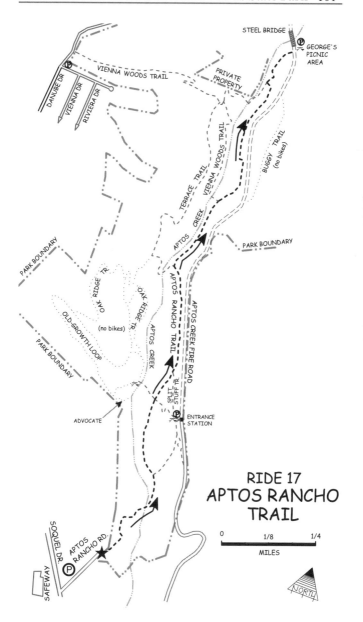

STEEL BRIDGE

GEORGE'S PICNIC AREA

VIENNA WOODS TRAIL

PRIVATE PROPERTY

DANUBE DR

VIENNA DR

RIVIERA DR

TERRACE TRAIL

VIENNA WOODS TRAIL

BUGGY TRAIL (no bikes)

APTOS CREEK

PARK BOUNDARY

PARK BOUNDARY

OAK RIDGE TR.

OAK RIDGE TR.

OLD-GROWTH LOOP

(no bikes)

APTOS RANCHO TRAIL

APTOS CREEK FIRE ROAD

APTOS CREEK

PARK BOUNDARY

SPLIT STUFF TR.

ENTRANCE STATION

ADVOCATE

RIDE 17
APTOS RANCHO
TRAIL

SOQUEL DR.

SAFEWAY

APTOS RANCHO RD.

0   1/8   1/4

MILES

NORTH

Directions/Access: From Santa Cruz, take Highway 1 South to the State Park Drive exit in Aptos, and head inland. Turn right onto Soquel Dr. Make a quick left onto Aptos Rancho Road (opposite Safeway). You will enter a residential area; park on the left side in front of the gate. To access the trailhead, ride 100 yards past the gate.

Mileage Guide	
0.0	Aptos Rancho Trailhead. Descend the wide at first singletrack.
.35	Aptos Creek crossing. The trail is just to the left on the other side of the creek.
.45	Trail splits; go straight (left). The trail to the right steeply climbs to the entrance booth on Aptos Creek Road. As you continue, ignore similar spur trails.
.60	Go straight through the intersection with the Old-Growth Loop Trail. The next short section of trail is a bit more challenging with roots and ruts. Charge!
.70	Stay straight as a trail enters on the left.
1.1	Pedal by the Terrace Trail off to the left.
1.2	Ignoring Vienna Woods Trail, continue up the hill.
1.5	Gnarly 3-foot ego-tester root drop!
1.6	Roll on by the upper section of Terrace Trail off to the left. (One possible loop option is to cross over the bridge here and follow Terrace Trail until it loops back to Aptos Rancho Trail).
1.9	George's Picnic Area.
2.0	Aptos Creek Road. The Steel Bridge is to your left. If you're riding this as an out & back, turn around and cruise back the way you came!
4.0	Back at the Aptos Rancho Trailhead.

Ride 18
Vienna Woods Combo Loop

The Vienna Woods Trail.

Location: Aptos; about 6 miles southeast of Santa Cruz.

Distance: 3.5 miles.

Elevation: 100/440 ft.

Trail Surface: 100% singletrack.

Type of Ride: Loop (figure-8) with an out & back section.

Terrain: Dense redwood forest; creek crossings.

Technical Level: Medium; the trail is often silky smooth, but watch out for a few surprise roots, drop-offs, log obstacles, and quick changes in elevation.

Exertion Level: Moderate; with a gradual and somewhat long climb out.

Highlights: This loop maximizes some of the best open singletrack within the lower Nisene trail network. It begins and ends on the Vienna Woods Trail and cruises along both the Terrace and Rancho Aptos Trails. As you cross Aptos Creek a few times, you'll pass plenty of mossy fern grottos and redwood trees. This ride will delight you with everything from smooth bermed corners to more technical segments.

Options: Try riding in different directions and/or add a longer section by riding all of Aptos Rancho Trail.

Note: There is a bridge at the upper Terrace Trail creek crossing, but not at either the Vienna or lower Terrace Trail crossings. However, there are often logs or rocks to aid in the crossing.

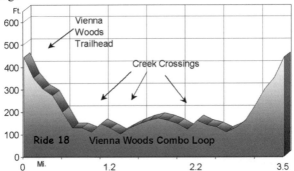

Directions/Access: From Santa Cruz, take Highway 1 South to Park Ave exit and head inland. In about .4 miles, turn right onto Soquel Drive. After 1 mile, make a left and head up Vienna Drive. In just under a mile, turn left on Wilshire Drive and make a quick right on Danube Drive. Park on the right hand side in front of the "Stop: Private Road" sign. The trailhead is about 20 feet beyond the sign on the right.

Mileage Guide	
0.0	The Vienna Woods Trailhead is about 20 feet up the private road " Mesa Grande Road" on the right.
.50	Ignore the shortcut trail on the right; keep straight.
.60	Major intersection! Keep going straight on Vienna Woods/Terrace Trail past the sign. About 200 feet ahead, make a sharp right onto the lower portion of Vienna Woods trail. While descending toward Aptos

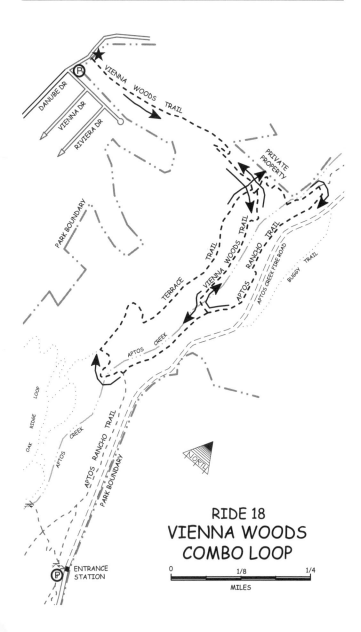

DANUBE DR

VIENNA DR

RIVIERA DR

VIENNA WOODS TRAIL

PRIVATE PROPERTY

PARK BOUNDARY

TERRACE TRAIL

VIENNA WOODS TRAIL

APTOS RANCHO TRAIL

APTOS CREEK FIRE ROAD

BUGGY TRAIL

APTOS CREEK

OAK RIDGE LOOP

APTOS CREEK

APTOS RANCHO TRAIL

PARK BOUNDARY

NORTH

ENTRANCE STATION

RIDE 18
VIENNA WOODS
COMBO LOOP

0   1/8   1/4
MILES

	Creek, ignore any spur trails off to the side.
.90	Creek crossing ahead. Ride up the bank on the other side, and turn right onto Aptos Rancho Trail.
1.1	Are you ready for another creek crossing yet? Turn right onto Terrace Trail and head for the creek.
1.2	After crossing the creek, find the trail in the midst of thick bushes. (Watch out for stinging nettles!)
1.4	When you come to the split in the trail, go right to continue on Terrace Trail.
1.7	Stay on the main trail and disregard all the spur trails coming down the bank.
1.9	Back to the major intersection again. Veer right and stay on Terrace Trail for a winding rollercoaster section of trail! (Pedal past the Vienna Woods Trail turnoff that is just ahead on the right).
2.1	Cross over the bridge and head up the bank toward Aptos Rancho Trail.
2.2	Go Right on Aptos Rancho Trail.
2.3	3-foot root!
2.6	Go right on the Vienna Woods Trail and cross the creek for the last time.
2.9	Head left at the split. As you quickly come to the next intersection, keep going straight on Vienna Woods Trail.
3.5	Back at the trailhead.

Fast, fun, downhill singletrack at the Vienna Woods Trailhead.

Getting' loose on the Vienna Woods Combo Loop

Ride 19
Aptos Creek Fire Road:
To Sand Point Overlook

Location: Aptos; 6 miles southeast of Santa Cruz.

Distance: 17 miles roundtrip.

Elevation: 160/1600 ft.

Trail Surface: 100% dirt & fire road.

Type of Ride: Out & Back.

Terrain: Shady young redwood forest; Aptos and Bridge Creeks; excellent ocean and ridge views.

Technical Level: Easy; it's a fairly smooth and wide road for the most part. Micro-ruts develop in the winter.

Exertion Level: Strenuous. The first 3.8 miles are easy, but the fire road steepens for the remaining 4.7 miles up to the overlook.

Highlights: This out and back ride is definitely one of the most popular in Santa Cruz! Riding while thoroughly immersed in nature, this is one of the most rewarding workouts

available. At Sand Point, you will be blessed with unforget-
table views of Santa Cruz and Monterey Bay.

Rewarding ocean views at Sand Point Overlook.

Options: Any length ride is possible. Families may opt to ride
the first 3 or so miles to one of the picnic areas. Rides can also
be lengthened by riding beyond the overlook to Santa Rosalia
Mountain (Ride 20), or riding a loop with Hinckley Basin Fire
Road (Ride 21). To gain some singletrack, ride up Aptos
Rancho Trail to the Steel Bridge (Ride 17).

Note: Mountain bikes are only allowed on the roads beyond
the Steel Bridge. Fines will be issued to those who ride any of

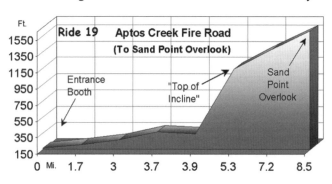

the coveted singletrack trails back down, particularly on West Ridge Trail. If enough cooperative mountain bikers voice their opinions to officials, however, trail policies could potentially change.

Directions/Access: From Santa Cruz, take Highway 1 south to State Park exit in Aptos. Go inland and take a right onto Soquel Drive. As you enter the Aptos Village area, make a left on Aptos Creek Road. You can park near the trailhead, just past the entrance booth ($1 when staffed). Or for a little longer ride, many people prefer to park behind the Aptos Station in town. The mileage guide for this ride begins just beyond the entrance booth where the pavement ends.

Crossing the steel bridge on the way down from Sand Point.

Mileage Guide	
0.0	Just beyond the entrance booth, the pavement on Aptos Creek Road gives way to packed dirt. The next 3.8 miles are a relatively easy ride.
1.1	Pass Aptos Rancho Trail and Georges Picnic Area.
1.2	Cross over the Steel Bridge.
1.5	Roll on by West Ridge Trailhead off to the left.
1.7	Next, you'll pass the Mary Easton Picnic area.

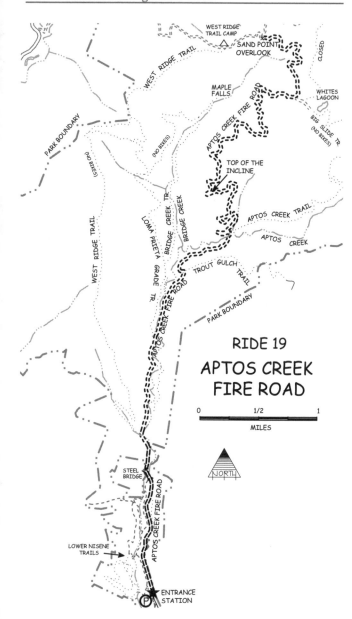

WEST RIDGE TRAIL CAMP

SAND POINT OVERLOOK

CLOSED

WEST RIDGE TRAIL

MAPLE FALLS

WHITES LAGOON

APTOS CREEK FIRE ROAD

BIG SLIDE TR. (NO BIKES)

PARK BOUNDARY

(NO BIKES)

TOP OF THE INCLINE

LOMA PRIETA GRADE TR.

BRIDGE CREEK TR.

BRIDGE CREEK

APTOS CREEK TRAIL

APTOS CREEK

WEST RIDGE TRAIL

APTOS CREEK FIRE ROAD

TROUT GULCH TRAIL

PARK BOUNDARY

RIDE 19
APTOS CREEK
FIRE ROAD

0   1/2   1
MILES

NORTH

STEEL BRIDGE

APTOS CREEK FIRE ROAD

LOWER NISENE TRAILS

ENTRANCE STATION

2.2	The road splits at the Porter Family Picnic area. Just ahead on the left, the official Aptos Creek Fire Road begins at the gate.
2.8	The historic Loma Prieta Mill Site is on the left.
3.8	Stay to the left after the bridge crossing (Aptos Creek Trail spurs off on the outside of the bend). Here, a panel describing the Loma Prieta Earthquake Epicenter marks the increase of the incline. From now on, the fire road will provide more of an intense workout.
5.3	You've reached the "Top of Incline." Don't get too excited quite yet; this refers to the historic logging operation and is not the top of the climb. Although, the road wont be quite as steep since it starts to follow the old railroad grade again.
7.5	Crank on by White's Lagoon Road/Big Slide Trail.
8.5	Sand Point Overlook! If it is clear, grandiose views await you! If you're eager for more elevation, continue on up to the right on upper Aptos Creek Fire Road (Ride 20). Another option is to take Hinckley Basin Fire Road (Ride 21), which is to your left. Passing West Ridge trail, it descends to Olive Springs Road and on to Old San Jose Road. However, most people opt to ride Aptos Creek Fire Road back down as an out & back ride.
17	By this point you should finally be cooled down from the climb! After one long descent, you are back at the entrance booth.

Ride 20
Upper Aptos Creek Fire Road:
Sand Point Overlook to Buzzard Lagoon Road

A view from upper Aptos Creek Fire Road.

Location: In the center of The Forest of Nisene Marks.

Distance: 3.4 miles one-way to Santa Rosalia Ridge Overlook; 5.8 miles to Buzzard Lagoon Road.

Elevation: 1600/2600 ft.

Trail Surface: 100% fire road.

Type of Ride: Out & Back.

Terrain: Redwood forest; mountain ridge; viewpoint.

Technical Level: Easy; fairly smooth and wide road for the most part.

Exertion Level: Strenuous. By this point you've already had a pretty good warm up; to say the least.

Highlights: For endurance maniacs, there are many more miles to tackle beyond Sand Point Overlook. With more great views and forest scenery, the ride takes you to one of the highest points in the county; Santa Rosalia Mountain near Soquel Demonstration Forest.

Options: Most riders simply bike to the Santa Rosalia Ridge Overlook as an out & back. Depending on where you rode in from, you can connect the ride with Hinckley Basin Fire Road (Ride 21), Lower Aptos Creek Fire Road (Ride 19), or Buzzard Lagoon Road. Also, from the Santa Rosalia viewpoint, you can descend into Soquel Demonstration Forest via sweet singletrack (see Ride 22).

Note: Just another reminder that bikes are officially allowed only on the dirt roads in this part of Nisene Marks.

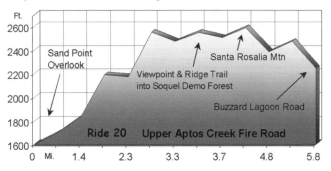

Directions/Access: Most people access this trail from the Nisene Marks main entrance in Aptos by riding up the lower section of Aptos Creek Fire Road. It can also be accessed from Hinckley Basin Fire Road commencing from Old San Jose Road, or from the opposite direction on Buzzard Lagoon Road in Corralitos, or from the Soquel Demonstration Forest.

Mileage Guide	
0.0	Sand Point Overlook. After taking in this magnificent viewpoint, start riding up Aptos Creek Fire Road by staying to the right.
1.3	Pedal by the closed bootleg trail known as the "Indy/Pig Trail."
2.5	A short unmarked viewpoint trail is on the right.

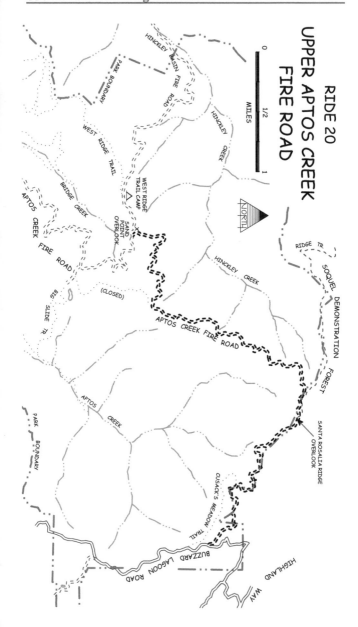

RIDE 20
UPPER APTOS CREEK
FIRE ROAD

3.4	Santa Rosalia Ridge Overlook. Great place to take a break or turn around. There's a tree-framed viewpoint on the right, and the Ridge Trail (Soquel Demonstration Forest) is on the left. If you're burning for more, keep heading up Santa Rosalia Mountain.
4.0	You'll pass a short alternate trail to the left.
4.2	The alternate trail reemerges here. Here, on Santa Rosalia Mountain, you are riding on some of the highest sections of trail in Santa Cruz. If this is not your final destination, you can keep exploring by riding down the fire road toward Buzzard Lagoon Road.
4.3	Just ahead is the gate to mark the official end of the Aptos Creek Fire Road. A tight trail on the left bypasses the gate.
4.7	At the bottom of the trough on the right, there is a frequently biked singletrack, Cusack's Meadow Trail, that ends on Buzzard Lagoon Road. Although many bikers utilize this trail, it is officially closed to bicycle use. Therefore, keep riding the main fire road.
5.8	Buzzard Lagoon Road. Turning left will head you in the direction of the Soquel Demonstration Forest entrance, via Highland Way. Turning right goes toward Buzzard Lagoon and the bottom of Cusack's Meadow Trail. And, of course, turning around takes you back the way you came.

A cloud burst viewed from the unmarked viewpoint off of upper Aptos Creek Fire Road.

Ride 21
Hinckley Basin Fire Road:
To Sand Point Overlook

Hinckley Road.

Location: Soquel; 4 miles southeast of Santa Cruz.

Distance: 3.2 miles each way.

Elevation: 360/1600 ft.

Trail Surface: 100% dirt road.

Type of Ride: Out & Back; or a segment in a loop.

Terrain: Forest; creek crossings.

Technical Level: Easy; a mostly smooth and wide road, but it has very steep sections.

Exertion Level: Very Strenuous; unless you're just bombing it downhill.

Highlights: This ride is a heck of a work out and a rarely utilized access to West Ridge Camp, Aptos Creek Fire Road, and Sand Point Overlook. At Sand Point, you will be treated with wonderful views of Santa Cruz and Monterey Bay.

Options: For a longer ride, keep biking up Aptos Creek Fire Rd (Ride 20). Some people ride beyond the Overlook to Santa Rosalia Mountain, or make a loop with the lower section of Aptos Creek Rd (Ride 19), Soquel Dr, and Old San Jose Rd.

Note: As you'll be cruising right past the West Ridge Trail, please remember that this is illegal for bikes. Don't look lest you be tempted.

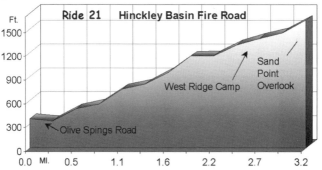

Directions/Access: Take Highway 1 North from Santa Cruz, and exit Bay/Porter St. Head inland and cross Soquel Dr. The street becomes Old San Jose Rd. Turn right and drive up Olive Springs Rd. Spot the gated dirt road on the right, across the road from the quarry staging area/weigh scale. Hinckley Basin Fire Rd is also accessed from Aptos Creek Fire Rd (Ride 19).

Mileage Guide	
0.0	From Olive Springs Road, turn right and pass around the gate labeled "Hinckley Road." The first .4 miles of the ride involves small creek crossings; be sure to spot the seasonal waterfall at the last crossing.
1.0	Ride by the private cabins off to the right.
1.2	As the road splits here; stay to the left.

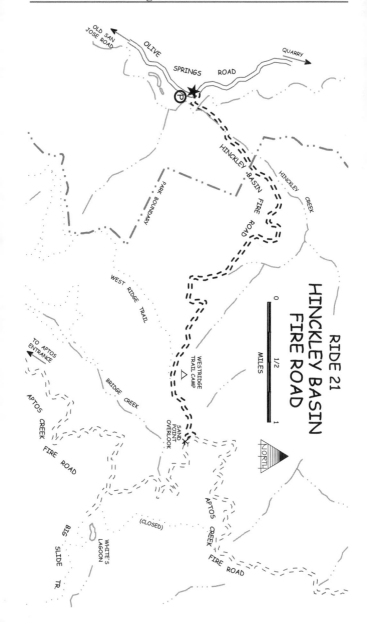

RIDE 21
HINCKLEY BASIN
FIRE ROAD

1.5	Again, stay left as you pedal by private property. Many private motorcycle trails spur off the road in this area.
1.7	Cruise around the gate ahead.
2.7	West Ridge Camp is on the left, and West Ridge Trail is on the right. Keep on cranking up.
3.2	Payoff time! Sand Point Overlook! After taking in the sights, you can either ride on Aptos Creek Fire Road or head back down Hinckley Road.
6.4	With no extra exploring, you'll be back at the Hinckley trailhead.

Ride 22
The Ultra Mega Nisene-Demo Ride

Location: Aptos, 6.5 miles southeast of Santa Cruz.

Distance: 32-33.5 miles, depending on options chosen.

Elevation: 150/2550 ft.

Trail Surface: 15% singletrack; 85% fire roads; more single-track options possible.

Type of Ride: Out & back with loop.

Terrain: Dense forest; creeks; ridges; mountains; great views.

Technical Level: Ranges from Easy to Very Difficult.

Exertion Level: Very Strenuous; extreme mega work out.

Highlights: Riding nearly from the coast to the 'summit' and back, this is a dream workout of epic proportions for the serious cross-country mountain biker (a.k.a. Hammerhead). With gut-wrenching uphills and kamikaze downhills, there are plenty of variety, great views, and challenge as you ride the length of both Nisene Marks and Soquel Demonstration forest!

Options: You can alternate some of the fire road sections for more singletrack, such as in the lower Nisene Marks area.

Note: Bring lots of food and water! Start early or bring a light!

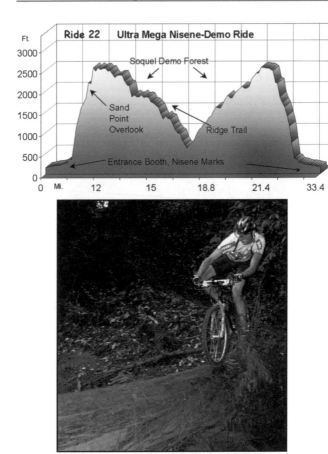

Going for it on a balance-testing log.

Directions/Access: See Ride 19.

Mileage Guide	
0.0	At the entrance booth, ride up Aptos Creek Road.
1.2	Steel bridge.
2.2	At the split, stay left and pass around the gate to continue riding up Aptos Creek Fire Road.
3.8	Get ready to start cranking as the trail steepens.

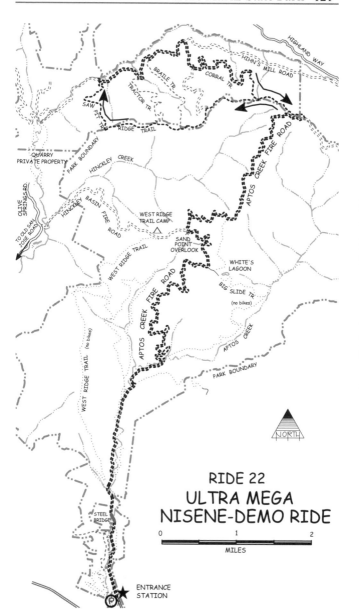

SAW PIT TR.
TRACTOR TR.
BRATLE TR.
CORRAL TR.
HIHN'S MILL ROAD
HIGHLAND WAY
RIDGE TRAIL
QUARRY
PRIVATE PROPERTY
OLIVE SPRINGS RD.
TO OLD SAN JOSE ROAD
PARK BOUNDARY
HINCKLEY CREEK
HINCKLEY BASIN FIRE ROAD
WEST RIDGE TRAIL CAMP
SAND POINT OVERLOOK
WHITE'S LAGOON
BIG SLIDE TR. (no bikes)
WEST RIDGE TRAIL
APTOS CREEK FIRE ROAD
APTOS CREEK FIRE ROAD
APTOS CREEK
PARK BOUNDARY
WEST RIDGE TRAIL (no bikes)
STEEL BRIDGE
ENTRANCE STATION

NORTH

RIDE 22
ULTRA MEGA
NISENE-DEMO RIDE

0   1   2
MILES

5.3	"Top of Incline." Enjoy the milder grade as the road follows the old railroad grade once again.
8.5	Sand Point Overlook! Spectacular place to catch your breath. When you're ready to endure more, stay to the right on Aptos Creek Fire Road and keep charging up!
11.9	Intersection with more ocean views on the right! Go left at the sign to ride Soquel Demo Forest's Ridge Trail! As you descend this rockin' trail, there will be 5 options to turn right and descend to Hihn Mill Road. The farther you go, the longer the loop! For detailed information on these trails see Rides 25 A-G.
12.5	Corral Trail is on the right (see Ride 25B).
13.5	Continuing on Ridge Trail, you will pass a helipad on the right. Just ahead is the second option; Sulphur Springs Trail (Ride 25C). Stay left if you decide to keep riding Ridge Trail.
14.0	Braille Trail (see 25D) is on the right.
14.5	Tractor Trail (see 25E) is next up. If you keep riding beyond on Ridge Trail, the next section will include some very steep and rutted out downhills.
15.4	Prepare for one gnarly uphill! Just afterwards is the end of the Ridge Trail. Turn right and descend Saw Pit Trail (25F).
16.7	After a great downhill section, turn right on Hihn Mill Road to start a gradual climb out.
17.3	On the right, you'll pass the bottom of Tractor Trail.
17.7	Keep chugging by Braille Trail.
18.6	Finally you'll come to Sulphur Springs Trail (dirt road). Go right and keep cranking.
18.7	Keep going straight, a road will merge on the right.
19.0	At the intersection go left on the Corral Trail, and begin a heart-thumping climb that will test your will.
20.3	The trail takes a sharp right-hand turn at the sign and becomes a very steep singletrack. Mere mortals have to

	settle with a section of 'hike-n-bike.'
20.8	Whoohooo! Ridge Trail! Turn left and pedal back to Nisene Marks. The remainder of the ride is an out & back.
21.5	Turn right on Aptos Creek Fire Road. Most of the rest of ride will be downhill; enjoy the speed!
24.9	Sand Point Overlook.
32.2	Steel Bridge.
33.4	Entrance Booth. How does a super-burrito sound?

Crossing Aptos Creek on Ride 18.

Soquel Demonstration State Forest

Singletrack that makes dreams come true.

Providing some of Santa Cruz's most challenging terrain, Soquel Demonstration State Forest offers almost 21 miles of mountain biking trails. Of these trails, 10 miles are epic single-track. Nestled between the Forest of Nisene Marks and upper Soquel Creek, the "Demo Forest's" topography is very steep. However, the exhilarating singletrack descents are well worth the grinding uphill sections.

Operated by the California Department of Forestry and Fire Protection, Soquel Demonstration Forest is used for forest management projects as well as recreation. It has no facilities, bathrooms, or formal parking. The main access area is located 6 miles east of Soquel-San Jose Road (Old San Jose Road) on Highland Way.

Ride 23
Outer Demo Loop

Uncrowded trails in the "Demo Forest."

Location: Bordering the northern boundary of Nisene Marks State Park, near the "Summit."

Distance: 12-15 miles.

Elevation: 1600/2600 ft.

Trail Surface: 40% singletrack; 47% dirt & fire roads; 13% paved road. (The amount of singletrack varies depending on the options chosen).

Type of Ride: Loop.

Terrain: Forest; ridgeline; steep terrain; views.

Technical Level: Difficult; steep downhill trails. However, it is possible to ride on almost all dirt roads, in which case it rates

Moderate.

Exertion Level: Strenuous.

Highlights: This Santa Cruz classic is a must-do ride! As one of the more challenging loops in Santa Cruz, you'll experience endorphin rushes from the invigorating climbs and pure down-hill bliss on insane singletrack. Don't forget to catch some glimpses of the awe-inspiring views!

Options: You can shorten or lengthen, and increase or decrease difficulty by choosing which trail to descend. See specific trail descriptions; Rides 25 A-F.

Note: This ride describes the longest possible loop; the full length of Ridge Trail to Saw Pit Trail. If you are a novice rider, you may want to take Sulphur Springs trail to avoid the tech-nical sections beyond. Also, keep in mind that most of the final jaunt on Hihn's Mill is uphill; the farther you ride down on the Ridge Trail, the farther you will have to climb out....it is way worth it though!

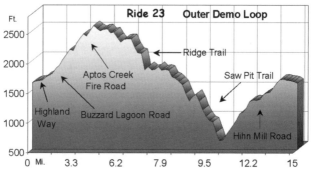

Directions/Access: From Santa Cruz or San Jose, take Highway 17 to the "Summit." Exit on the east side on Summit Dr (from Santa Cruz, this will be on the right). You will be on this road for about 10 miles. When the road forks, stay on Highland Way; (after the stop sign, you will veer right, and at the next split stay left). As the road descends into the valley, look on the right for the dirt pull-out and a small green sign that says "Soquel Demonstration State Forest." You'll see a bridge with bright yellow railing over the creek. Park here or drive across the bridge and park in the dirt pullout area on the right. (Don't leave valuables in your car here!) Soquel Demonstration Forest can also be reached by taking Soquel-San Jose Rd (Old San Jose Rd) from Soquel; turn right on Highland Way and drive 6 miles east.

Descending the Ridge Trail.

Mileage Guide	
0.0	From the dirt parking area by the yellow bridge, ride east (up the canyon) on Highland Way.
2.0	At the top, turn right on Buzzard Lagoon Road (dirt).
2.5	Buzzard Lagoon Road makes a sharp left turn here. Just ahead, you will enter the Forest of Nisene Marks beyond the gate.
3.0	At the road split, turn right onto the fire road and keep cranking. This becomes Aptos Creek Fire Road. (You may see bikers continue riding on Buzzard Lagoon Road to Cusack's Meadow Trail for more singletrack. Although this trail is often ridden by bikers, it is officially closed and off limits to bikes.)

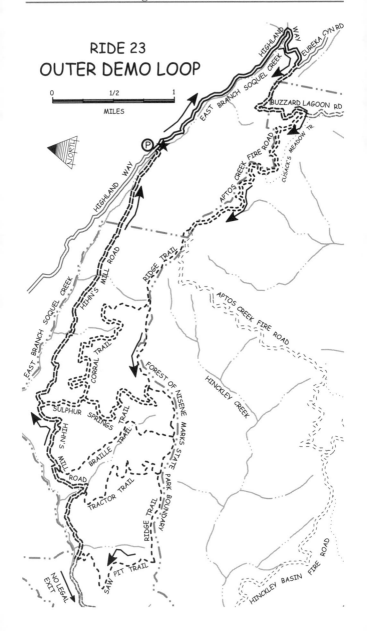

RIDE 23
OUTER DEMO LOOP

0   1/2   1
MILES

NORTH

HIGHLAND WAY

EUREKA CYN RD

EAST BRANCH SOQUEL CREEK

BUZZARD LAGOON RD

CUSACK'S MEADOW TR.

APTOS CREEK FIRE ROAD

P

HIGHLAND WAY

HIHN'S MILL ROAD

RIDGE TRAIL

EAST BRANCH SOQUEL CREEK

CORRAL TRAIL

APTOS CREEK FIRE ROAD

HINCKLEY CREEK

FOREST OF NISENE MARKS STATE PARK BOUNDARY

SULPHUR SPRINGS TRAIL

HIHN'S MILL ROAD

BRAILLE TRAIL

TRACTOR TRAIL

RIDGE TRAIL

SAW PIT TRAIL

NO LEGAL EXIT

HINCKLEY BASIN FIRE ROAD

3.8	Ignore the private maintenance road/trail on the right. How about a little downhill relief now!?
4.0	At the bottom of the trough, you will pass the top of Cusack's Meadow Trail (no bikes). Continue up the fire road.
4.3	Nisene Marks gate; this is where the road officially becomes Aptos Creek Fire Road. (100 feet below, a tight trail bypasses the gate).
4.5	As you continue up the fire road, you'll see a short alternate trail on the right. Soon its all downhill!
5.3	At the green sign, the Ridge Trail descends on the right. Before bombing down this insane singletrack, you can revitalize your soul with the tree-framed vistas of the bay! As you head down Ridge Trail, there will progressively be five options to turn right and descend back to Hihn's Mill Road which will ultimately take you to your car. (See Rides 25 A-F for more details on this section of trail).
5.9	Corral Trail is on the right (see 25B).
6.8	Continuing on Ridge Trail, you will pass by a helipad off to the right. Just ahead is the second option; Sulphur Springs Trail (see 25C). Stay left if you decide to keep riding Ridge Trail.
7.3	Braille Trail (See 25D) is on the right.
7.8	Tractor Trail (see 25E) is next up. If you keep riding beyond on Ridge, the next section will include some very steep and rutted out downhill sections.
8.7	Now that you descended all that way, prepare for one insane-in-the-membrane (but somewhat short) uphill climb! You can make it....charge!
8.8	This is the end of the Ridge Trail. Your last option is to turn right on Saw Pit Trail (see 25F).
10.0	After that permagrin-inducing downhill, turn right on Hihn's Mill Road to start a long climb back.
10.6	On the right, you'll pass the bottom of Tractor Trail.
11.0	Keep chugging by Braille Trail.

11.9	Next you'll pass Sulphur Springs Trailhead.
14.9	Yellow gate.
15.0	Cross yellow-railed bridge to your car.

Ride 24
Inner Demo Loop

There are plenty of challenging diversions on the Braille Trail.

Location: North of Nisene Marks near the "Summit."

Distance: 12-13.5 miles.

Elevation: 1600/2600 ft.

Trail Surface: 35% singletrack; 65% fire road. (Amount

depends on the options you choose).

Type of Ride: Loop.

Terrain: Dense forest; steep mountain riding.

Technical Level: Most Difficult; lots of climbing and steep descents on the singletrack sections.

Exertion Level: Very Strenuous.

Highlights: This is an extreme ride with steep uphills and steep downhills! With plenty of options to keep you stoked, many hardcore riders will do multiple loops! Ride up Corral Trail or Sulphur Springs Trail, and then descend down Ridge Trail to Braille, Tractor, or Saw Pit Trails.

Options: You can shorten, lengthen, increase, or decrease difficulty by choosing which trail to descend or ascend. Please see Rides 25 A-F.

Note: For intermediate level riders at least.

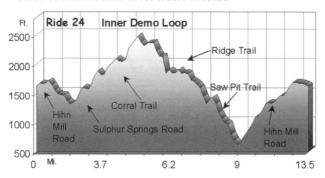

Directions/Access: See Ride 23.

Mileage Guide	
0.0	From Highland Way parking area, cross the yellow-railed bridge and head up Hihn's Mill Road.
.20	Pass around the yellow gate and the information panel on the right.
2.5	Turn left at Sulphur Springs Trail (dirt road).

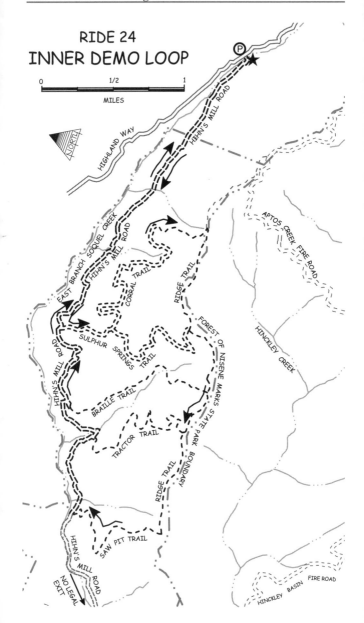

RIDE 24
INNER DEMO LOOP

0   1/2   1

MILES

NORTH

HIGHLAND WAY

HIHN'S MILL ROAD

P

APTOS CREEK FIRE ROAD

EAST BRANCH SOQUEL CREEK

HIHN'S MILL ROAD

CORRAL TRAIL

RIDGE TRAIL

HINCKLEY CREEK

HIHN'S MILL ROAD

SULPHUR SPRINGS TRAIL

FOREST OF NISENE MARKS STATE PARK

BRAILLE TRAIL

TRACTOR TRAIL

RIDGE TRAIL

BOUNDARY

HIHN'S MILL ROAD

NO LEGAL EXIT

SAW PIT TRAIL

HINCKLEY BASIN FIRE ROAD

2.7	Keep going straight; a road will merge on the right.
2.9	Corral Trail splits off Sulphur Springs to the left (straight). Both ways have very steep sections as they ascend to the ridge trail. To maximize singletrack riding, take Corral Trail.
4.2	The Corral Trail takes a sharp right turn at the sign and becomes a very steep singletrack. You're either lying or you're Superman if you can make it to the top without walking. This next section is tough!
4.7	Ridge Trail. You can breathe now! Turn right and start your descent. (There are some short uphill sections). As you ride Ridge Trail, there are four trail choices to turn right on.
5.6	Pass by the helipad on the right. Just ahead is Sulphur Springs Trail (see 25C). Stay left to keep riding Ridge Trail.
6.1	The world-famous Braille Trail (see 25D) is on the right.
6.5	Tractor Trail (see 25E) is next up. Beyond this point, Ridge Trail has some very steep and rutted out downhill sections.
7.5	If your cheeks hurt from grinning, you can give them a break as you grunt up this next very steep section. This will take you to the end of the Ridge Trail. Turn right to bomb Saw Pit Trail (see 25F). Yeehaaa!
8.8	Go right on Hihn's Mill Road to start a long gradual climb back.
9.5	Pass by Tractor Trail.
9.8	Next you'll pass by Braille Trail.
10.7	Keep cranking by Sulphur Springs Trailhead.
13.1	Yellow gate.
13.5	Cross yellow-railed bridge and head back to your car.

The yellow railed bridge marks the entrance to the park.

Rides 25 A-I
The Demo Forest Trail Guide

25A. Ridge Trail

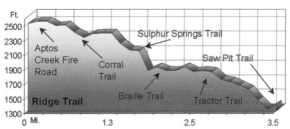

Distance: 3.5 miles.

Sections: .65 mi. from Ridge Trailhead to Corral; .95 mi. from Corral to Sulphur Springs; .5 mi. from Sulphur Springs to Braille; .5 mi. from Braille to Tractor; .9 mi. from Tractor to Saw Pit.

Elevation: 1320/2520 ft.

Trail Surface: 100% singletrack.

Technical Level: Ranges from Difficult to Most Difficult.

Exertion Level: Moderate going downhill. If for some reason you ride this uphill, it rates Very Strenuous.

Highlights: One of the most fun sections of downhill in the county! Fast, challenging, sometimes very technical, great views!

The following trails 25 B-F descend perpendicularly from Ridge Trail to Hihn's Mill Road:

25B. Corral Trail

Distance: 1.8 miles; 2.2 miles including bottom of Sulphur Springs Trail.

Distance from Ridge Trailhead to top of Trail: .65 miles.

Distance from Sulphur Springs Trail bottom on Hihn's Mill Rd to entrance parking: 2.5 miles.

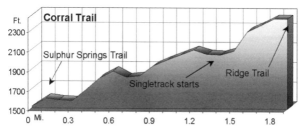

Elevation: 1520/2420 ft.

Trail Surface: 28% singletrack; 72% dirt road.

Technical Level: Difficult; due to a steep singletrack section on top.

Exertion Level: Very Strenuous; mega steep singletrack section in the last ½ mile.

Highlights: Great trail to climb up to access Ridge Trail. Also ridden for bomber high-speed descents.

25C. Sulphur Springs Trail

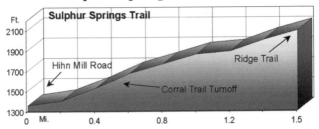

Distance: 1.5 miles.

Distance from Ridge Trailhead to top of Trail: 1.6 miles.

Distance from Trail bottom on Hihn's Mill Rd to entrance parking: 2.5 miles.

Elevation: 1350 /2200 ft.

Trail Surface: 100% dirt road.

Technical Level: Moderate; mostly smooth but very steep.

Exertion Level: Very Strenuous climbing uphill.

Highlights: Another great trail to climb up to access Ridge Trail due to its less technical dirt road status. Also a good way down for riders who prefer speed over technical challenge.

25D. Braille Trail

Distance: 1.6 miles.

Distance from Ridge Trailhead to top of Trail: 2.1 miles.

Distance from Trail bottom on Hihn's Mill Rd to entrance parking: 3.4 miles.

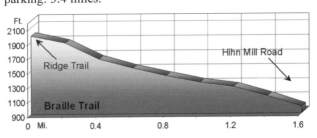

Elevation: 1000/1990 ft.

Trail Surface: 100% singletrack.

Technical Level: Most Difficult; a few very steep sections with some free-riding obstacles, although it is easy to ride around and avoid them.

Exertion Level: Moderate; while descending.

Highlights: What used to be one of the best kept secrets in Santa Cruz, is now one of the newest and most fun trails in the county! Full of steep shoots, jumps, logs, see-saws, banking turns, and vertical drops, this trail is a skill-testing downhill park. There are enough bailouts for all levels, however.

Just another day in the Soquel Demonstration State Forest.

25E.   Tractor Trail

Distance: 1.6 miles.

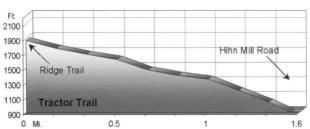

Distance from Ridge Trailhead to top of Trail: 2.6 miles.
Distance from Trail bottom on Hihn's Mill Rd to entrance parking: 3.9 miles.

Elevation: 850/1870 ft.

Trail Surface: 100% singletrack.

Technical Level: Difficult; some very steep sections.

Exertion Level: Very Strenuous when ascending.

Highlights: Steep at first; but lots of groovy turns, fast straight-aways, and jumps. The fun factor is very high on this trail!

25F. Saw Pit Trail

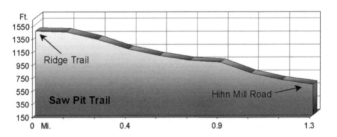

Distance: 1.25 miles.
Distance from Ridge Trailhead to top of Trail: 3.5 miles.
Distance from Trail bottom on Hihn's Mill Rd to entrance parking: 4.5 miles.

Elevation: 620/1400 ft.

Trail Surface: 100% singletrack.

Technical level: Most Difficult; steep sections.

Exertion Level: Strenuous when riding uphill.

Highlights: Another insane redwood forest trail with long steep descents. Riding this trail involves riding the full length of the Ridge Trail and thus maximizes the most downhill singletrack in the park. Don't forget it drops you way down Hihn's Mill Road with a relatively long ride back to the entrance.

25G. Hihn's Mill Road

Distance: 6 miles one-way; 5 miles to Badger Springs.

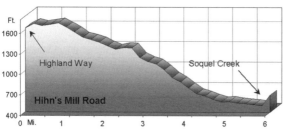

Elevation: 480/1690 ft.

Trail Surface: 100% dirt road.

Technical Level: Easy.

Exertion Level: Strenuous.

Highlights: Paralleling Soquel Creek, this road is most often used to access the singletrack trails. It is also a good out & back workout ride away from the crowds. Hihn's Mill passes Badger Springs picnic area, accesses Long Ridge Road and Amaya Creek Road, and has a bridge crossing over Soquel Creek.

Feelin' the need for speed on the Ridge Trail.

25H. Amaya Road

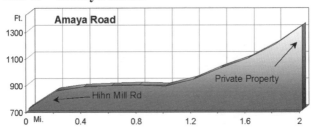

Distance: 2 miles one-way; ends at private property.

Elevation: 500/1250 ft.

Trail Surface: 100% dirt road.

Technical Level: Easy.

Exertion Level: Strenuous.

Highlights: If you are die-hard and want to add a few more uphill miles to Hihn's Mill Road, this is for you.

25I. Long Ridge Road

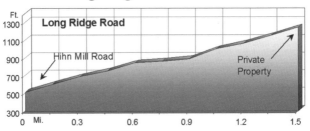

Distance: 1.5 miles one-way, before reaching private property.

Elevation: 510/1250 ft.

Trail Surface: 100% dirt road.

Technical Level: Easy.

Exertion Level: Strenuous.

Highlights: Accessed off Hihn's Mill Road just after Badger Springs, this road tacks mileage onto the lists of bike trails.

Big Basin Redwoods State Park

*Berry Creek Falls is a short hike off the
Waddell Creek/Skyline To The Sea Trail.*

Big Basin is destined to awe-inspire all who bike there.
Formed in 1902, Big Basin is California's oldest State Park. It
consists of over 18,000 acres of redwood, conifer, oak, and
chaparral, and contains the largest forest of "ancient coast"
redwoods south of San Francisco. The park stretches from sea
level to over 2,000 feet with everything from lush canyon bot-
toms to sparse chaparral-covered slopes. In addition, Big Basin
has several waterfalls; one of the most dramatic falls is a short

hike off the Waddell Creek bike ride. Even though Big Basin has over 80 miles of trails, only the fire roads are open to mountain bikes. These multi-use roads, however, cover an immense amount of terrain making for some excellent biking!

Maps and multimedia information are available at the park headquarters and the Sempervirens Room. Several camp-grounds, including bike assessable trail camps, are located throughout the park. The main park area is 22 miles northwest of Santa Cruz via Highways 9 and 236. The Waddell Creek/Skyline to the Sea Trail is located 13 miles northwest of Santa Cruz on Highway 1.

A northern Santa Cruz County beach visible on the way up to Waddell Creek and Big Basin State Park.

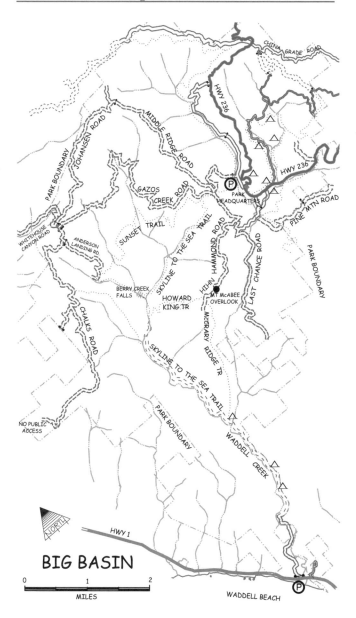

BIG BASIN

Ride 26
Waddell Creek/Skyline To The Sea Trail

Location: 13 miles north of Santa Cruz on Highway 1.

Distance: 11.8 miles.

Elevation: 20/320 ft.

Trail Surface: Mostly narrow fire road; (it has naturally eroded into singletrack in some sections).

Type of Ride: Out & Back.

Terrain: Beach; forest; creeks; waterfall.

Technical Level: Easy; with some more moderate sections where the road has become more of a trail.

Exertion Level: Mild; very gradual climb.

Highlights: This is an excellent family adventure for all ability levels! Starting at Waddell beach, this ride begins in the open sun before cruising along Waddell Creek in the moist lush forest. At the end of the ride, there is a ¾ mile hike up to one of Santa Cruz's most fabulous waterfalls! A bike rack area accompanies the trailhead; don't forget your bike lock!

Where the biking ends and the hike to Berry Creek Falls begins.

Options: Don't miss the Berry Creek Falls hike at the top of the bike ride.

Note: Biking is only allowed on fire roads. A $100+ fine will greet anyone poaching the hiking trails.

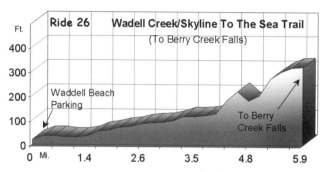

Directions/Access: From Santa Cruz, take Highway 1 North. After passing Western Drive, the last stoplight in Santa Cruz, it is about 9 ½ miles to Waddell Creek. After crossing over the creek, park at the beach parking on either side. The trailhead is on the inland side of Highway 1 from the Waddell Beach parking lot. Start at the gated paved entrance road.

Mileage Guide	
0.0	On the paved entrance road, ride around the gate and the information panel. There is a sign labeled "Skyline to the Sea Trail."
.40	Stay on the main road after passing the ranger station. After you ride around another gate, the road will become dirt.
.65	Ignore the road merging on the right.
1.1	Cross the bridge and pass by the private property.
1.7	Soon you'll ride by two of the trail camp areas.
3.0	This next section has some steeper singletrack switchbacks; the most technical portion of the ride.
3.2	Pass another trail camp.

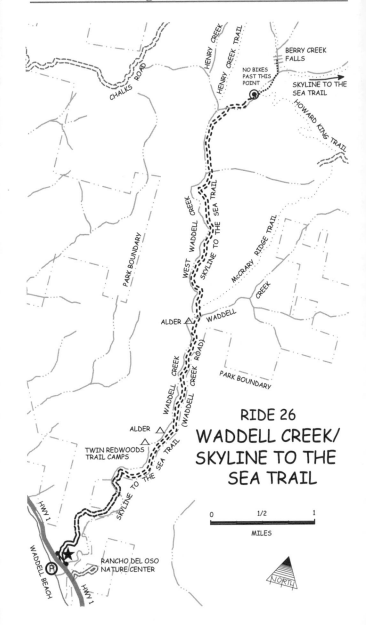

BERRY CREEK
FALLS

HENRY CREEK

HENRY CREEK TRAIL

NO BIKES
PAST THIS
POINT

SKYLINE TO THE
SEA TRAIL

CHALKS ROAD

HOWARD KING TRAIL

WEST WADDELL CREEK

SKYLINE TO THE SEA TRAIL

McCRARY RIDGE TRAIL

CREEK

PARK BOUNDARY

ALDER

WADDELL

WADDELL CREEK

(WADDELL CREEK ROAD)

PARK BOUNDARY

ALDER

TWIN REDWOODS
TRAIL CAMPS

SKYLINE TO THE SEA TRAIL

HWY 1

WADDELL BEACH

HWY 1

RANCHO DEL OSO
NATURE CENTER

RIDE 26
WADDELL CREEK/
SKYLINE TO THE
SEA TRAIL

0   1/2   1
MILES

NORTH

3.3	Turn right on the trail just before you get to the Waddell Creek crossing. This will take you onto the bridge and back to the main trail.
4.9	Bridge crossing.
5.5	Stay to the right on the main road.
5.7	Another bridge crossing.
5.9	End of the line for bikes! Park your bike in the bike racks and prepare for a little hike to a big waterfall! The trail is just to the right of the information panel and crosses the creek on a small footbridge. When you finish the hike, turn around and ride back down the same way.
11.8	Back at Waddell parking lot.

Waddell Beach; a popular surfing and kiteboarding/windsurfing spot on the border of Big Basin.

Ride 27
Big Basin Loop

A redwood scene from a bikers point of view on the Big Basin loop.

Location: 25 miles northwest of Santa Cruz.

Distance: 13.2 miles; more with spur options.

Elevation: 880/2030 ft.

Trail Surface: 94% fire road; 6% paved road.

Type of Ride: Loop.

Terrain: Redwood forest; lots of small creeks; views!

Technical Level: Medium; some steep sections with occasional ruts and bumpy sandstone rocks.

Exertion Level: Very Strenuous; this rating is based upon the first few miles which have some very steep heart-pounding segments. The climb out is far more gradual.

Highlights: Not only is this a great workout with incredible scenery, it has plenty of remote, fast and furious downhill sections! Majestic mountain and ocean views, an abundance of creeks, and plenty of magnificent redwoods will stoke you the whole way!

Options: There are several other out & back spur roads to explore as well.

Note: Biking is not allowed on any singletrack trails.

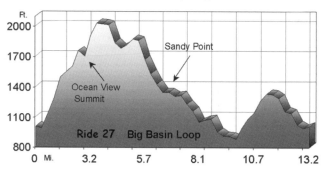

Directions/Access: From Santa Cruz, take Highway 9 (at the intersection of River St and Highway 1) 13 miles into Boulder Creek. Turn left on Highway 263 and take it for 9 miles to the park headquarters. Park in the lot across from the headquarters; (there is a small day-use fee).

Mileage Guide	
0.0	From the parking booth, ride north through the parking lot and pass the snack bar and nature lodge.
.30	Go left over the wood bridge and keep straight.
.40	Pedal around the brown gate as you ride up the canyon on Gazos Creek Road.
.50	The road now becomes dirt!
1.3	Go right on Middle Ridge Road and mentally prepare for some very steep sections ahead.
2.4	If you're starting to feel more sun and see open vistas, you are probably near Ocean View Summit! Great place to take a break before cranking on.
3.5	More great views from the ridge.
3.7	Gate.

PARK BOUNDARY

JOHANSEN ROAD

RIDE 27
BIG BASIN LOOP

0 — 1/2 — 1

MILES

NORTH

GAZOS CREEK ROAD

MIDDLE RIDGE ROAD

WEST WADDELL CREEK

GAZOS CREEK ROAD

OCEAN VIEW SUMMIT

SUNSET TRAIL

KELLY CREEK

SKYLINE TO THE SEA TRAIL

GAZOS CREEK ROAD

SKYLINE TO THE SEA TRAIL

NORTH ESCAPE ROAD

HIHN HAMMOND ROAD

HWY 236

LAST CHANCE ROAD

EAST WADDELL CREEK

P

PARK HEADQUARTERS

SEQUOIA

3.8	Go left at the intersection onto Johansen Road.
4.2	There will be more great views from the ridge.
4.4	Gate.
6.6	Pass around the big gate and go left on Gazos Creek Road. Shortly, take another left and ride around the gate as you continue on Gazos Creek Road.
7.2	Spectacular ridge, mountain, and ocean views here!
8.8	Lots of small creeks in this area; look out for waterfalls in the rainy season.
9.7	Gate.
10.3	The next mile and half will be a long but gradual uphill.
11.7	Downhill for the rest of the ride now!
11.9	Stay on the main road as you pass by other spur roads.
12.9	Turn right after crossing over the wood bridge.
13.2	End of the ride.

Gazos Creek Road has a few sections of Moab-like sandstone in dense redwood forests with ocean views.

Rides 28 A-H
Big Basin Trail Guide

28A. Gazos Creek Road

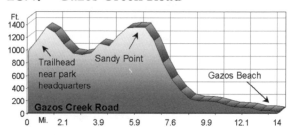

Distance: 14 miles.

Elevation: 20/1350 ft.

Trail Surface: 62 % dirt road; 38 % paved road.

Terrain: Dense forest; lots of creeks; some views; various strange bright orange sulphur-smelling springs.

Technical Level: Easy.

Exertion Level: Moderate/Strenuous.

Highlights: Gazos Creek Road cruises from the park headquarters all the way to Gazos beach. Some people ride the entire road as a one-way shuttle ride.

28B. Middle Ridge Road

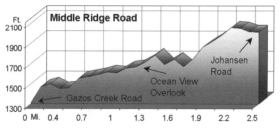

Distance: 2.5 miles.

Elevation: 1314/2050 ft.

Trail Surface: 100% dirt road.

Terrain: Forest; mountain ridge; ocean views.

Technical Level: Medium; some rocky sections.

Exertion Level: Very Strenuous; riding uphill.

Highlights: Connecting Gazos Creek and Johansen Roads, Middle Ridge Road has some fun and challenging sections. "Ocean View Summit" is about half way up.

28C. Hihn Hammond Road

Distance: 2.7 miles; 2 miles to the overlook.

Elevation: 1310/1730 ft.

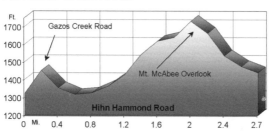

Trail Surface: 100% dirt road.

Terrain: Forest; overlook.

Technical Level: Medium.

Exertion Level: Moderate.

Highlights: At 2 miles, the Mt McAbee Overlook provides great views.

28D. Last Chance Road

Distance: 2.7 miles.

Elevation: 660/1290 ft.

Trail Surface: 100% dirt road.

Terrain: Forest; creek crossing.

Technical Level: Moderate.

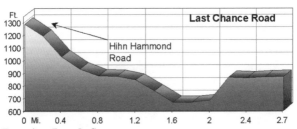

Exertion Level: Strenuous.

Highlights: This road winds along East Waddell Creek.

28E. Johansen Road

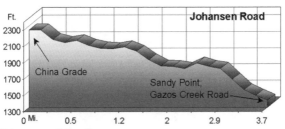

Distance: 3.7 miles.

Elevation: 1380/2250 ft.

Trail Surface: 100% dirt road.

Terrain: Dense forest; mountain views.

Technical Level: Easy.

Exertion Level: Very Strenuous if you ride uphill.

Highlights: Dropping from the north end of the park to Gazos Creek Road, Johansen Road contains one long fun downhill section when riding south.

28F. Whitehouse Canyon Road

Distance: 2.8 miles.

Elevation: 950/1350 ft.

Trail Surface: 100% dirt road.

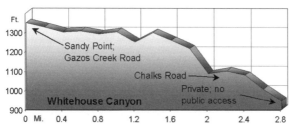

Terrain: Forest.

Technical Level: Medium.

Exertion Level: Moderate.

Highlights: There is also a 2.4-mile bottom section with public access off Highway 1, just south of Rossi Road. This takes you to an "unmaintained" double track and a hiking trail to a viewpoint.

28G. Anderson Landing Road

Distance: 1.1 miles one-way.

Elevation: 920/1340 ft.

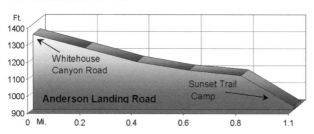

Trail Surface: 100% dirt road.

Terrain: Dense forest; ridge; view area.

Technical Level: Easy.

Exertion Level: Moderate.

Highlights: Anderson Landing Road spurs off Whitehouse Canyon Road and heads down to Sunset Trail Camp.

28H. Chalks Road

Distance: 3.4 miles; 1.5 miles to Chalk Mountain.

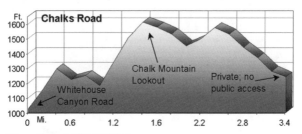

Elevation: 1030/1610 ft.

Trail Surface: 100% dirt road.

Terrain: Forest; viewpoint.

Technical Level: Medium.

Exertion Level: Strenuous.

Highlights: This road heads up to Chalk Mountain; a spectacular lookout just above "The Chalks." Here, Westridge hiking trail descends toward Waddell Beach.

Saratoga Gap/Long Ridge Open Space Preserves

Is it the trail or the ocean views that are so breathtaking?

Located on the northern boundary of Santa Cruz County, Saratoga Gap and Long Ridge Open Space Preserves are filled with gorgeous scenery and great mountain biking. Meandering through forest and ocean-framed grasslands, the riding is a fun mix-mash of trails and fire roads. Due to the amount of singletrack, amazing views, and proximity to the San Jose area, the open space preserves are very popular and can be rather crowded on weekends. However, these bike parks are definitely worth the trip!

In addition to the rides featured in this book, mountain bikers can enjoy many more miles of riding beyond Long Ridge and Saratoga Gap. These open spaces are linked to Upper Stevens Creek County Park, Skyline Ridge Open Space Preserve, and a series of other preserves and parks in the south Skyline region.

The trailhead is on the northeast quadrant of the junction of Highway 9 and Skyline Blvd (Highway 35). There are no bathrooms or water available. Trails are open from 8 am until sunset.

Ride 29
Saratoga Gap Trail

Biking under a forested canopy on the Saratoga Gap Trail.

Location: At the junction of Highway 9 and Skyline Blvd.

Distance: 4.4 miles.

Elevation: 2490/2690 ft.

Trail Surface: 100% singletrack.

Type of Ride: Out & Back.

Terrain: Shady forest with a section through grasslands.

Technical Level: Easy/Medium; trail is mostly smooth with various rocks and roots, and never too steep.

Exertion Level: Moderate; short gradual climbs/descents.

Highlights: If you want a short ride with lots of 'ups' and 'downs' on smooth singletrack; look no further. Advanced bikers may want to continue riding on the Bay Area Ridge Trail, but the Saratoga Gap Trail is a great out & back ride for beginners and intermediates.

Options: It is possible to keep riding as far as you want. See Ride 30 for more thrills.

Note: This is a high-use trail; ride accordingly.

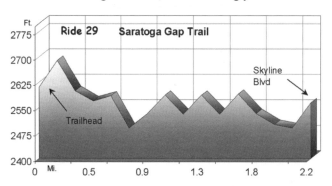

Directions/Access: From Santa Cruz, take Highway 9 all the way to Skyline Blvd (Highway 35) on the border of Santa Clara County. The trailhead is on the northeast side of the intersection. Parking is available directly in front of the trailhead or in the adjacent parking lot.

Mileage Guide	
0.0	Start riding up from the Saratoga Gap Trailhead.
1.8	Take the singletrack to the left as you reach the intersection area.
2.2	Skyline Blvd. The trail continues on the other side if you want to keep riding (Ride 30). Otherwise, turn around to ride back.
4.4	Back at the trailhead.

COUNTY PARK

OPEN SPACE PRESERVE

CHARCOAL ROAD

SARATOGA GAP TRAIL

OPEN SPACE PRESERVE

SANTA CLARA COUNTY

HWY 35

SANTA CRUZ COUNTY

SARATOGA GAP TRAIL

SKYLINE BOULEVARD

HWY 9

NORTH

RIDE 29
SARATOGA GAP TRAIL

0   1/4   1/2

MILES

Ride 30
Long Ridge Loop

Revitalizing the soul in Long Ridge Open Space Preserve.

Location: The junction of Highway 9 and Skyline Blvd.

Distance: 10.7 miles; more possible.

Elevation: 2160/2670 ft.

Trail Surface: 66% singletrack; 34% fire road.

Type of Ride: Loop with an out & back section.

Terrain: Ocean views; grasslands; forest; creek.

Technical Level: Medium.

Exertion Level: Moderate.

Highlights: One minute you'll be cruising through a lush oak, fir, and madrone forest; then suddenly you find yourself awestruck as you gaze over pristine grasslands bounded by Santa Cruz county and the Pacific Ocean. The ocean vistas are simply incredible…and all seen while riding smooth single-track and fire road.

Options: Many more miles can be tacked on by riding the Bay Area Ridge Trail beyond the Long Ridge/Peter's Creek intersection. Some people also do a larger and much steeper loop with Grizzly Flat Trail and Charcoal Road. This is only recommended if you love fast downhill descents followed by a relentless uphill section.

Note: Nice weekends bring lots of people to the trails; please be aware of others as you ride.

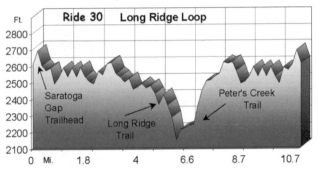

Directions/Access: See Direction/Access on Ride 29.

Mileage Guide	
0.0	Start riding up from the Saratoga Gap Trailhead.
1.8	At the intersection, veer left onto the singletrack.
2.2	Cross Skyline Blvd and continue on the Hickory Oaks Trail, which soon becomes a fire road.
2.4	Go left on the trail at the split. Mind blowing views ahead! (This is the kind of trail that inspires poetry and causes people to fall in love!)
2.7	At the fire road, go left.
3.3	At the split with Ward Road, veer right onto the singletrack.
3.5	Soon you will merge straight onto the dirt road.
3.6	Intersection of Ward Road, Peter's Creek Trail, and Long Ridge Road. Go straight on Long Ridge Road.
4.1	At the gate, go right on some sweeeet singletrack!

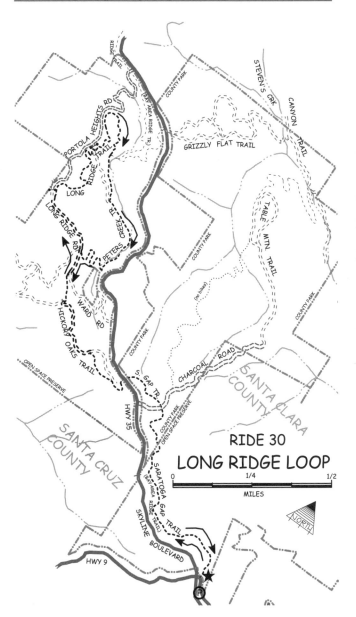

RIDGE TRAIL

STEVEN'S CRK CANYON TRAIL

(BA) AREA RIDGE TR)

COUNTY PARK

PORTOLA HEIGHTS RD

GRIZZLY FLAT TRAIL

LONG RIDGE TRAIL

COUNTY PARK

LONG RIDGE RD

PETERS CREEK RD

TABLE MTN. TRAIL

(no bikes)

COUNTY PARK

HICKORY OAKS TRAIL

WARD RD

CHARCOAL ROAD

SANTA CLARA COUNTY

OPEN SPACE PRESERVE

COUNTY PARK

S GAP TR.

HWY 35

COUNTY PARK
OPEN SPACE PRESERVE

RIDE 30
LONG RIDGE LOOP

0   1/4   1/2
MILES

SANTA CRUZ COUNTY

SARATOGA GAP (BA) AREA RIDGE TRAIL

SKYLINE BOULEVARD

SARATOGA GAP TRAIL

HWY 9

NORTH

P

4.9	Ignoring the road on the right, keep going straight.
5.6	After a rather steep downhill section, you reach Peters Creek Trail. Keep going straight here. (To extend this ride, go left. Options include riding the Ridge Trail, or making a far more strenuous loop with Grizzly Flat Trail (road), Canyon Trail, Table Mountain Trail, and Charcoal Road. See map.)
6.0	Stay on the trail as you pass a road up to the right.
6.7	The trail will curve around to the right and cross over a small bridge. Soon you will encounter a series of uphill switchbacks.
7.1	Back at the intersection with Long Ridge Road. Go left. The rest of the ride is an out and back.
7.2	Merge onto the trail.
7.4	Head left onto the dirt road.
8.0	Veer right onto the trail.
8.3	Go right on the short section of dirt road.
8.5	Cross Skyline Blvd and continue on the trail.
8.9	At the intersection, go straight onto the singletrack.
10.7	End of the line at the trailhead.

Bombing the Long Ridge Loop.

Access   Trails & Bike Paths

*A rest spot on the West Cliff Path with a
natural bridge in the background.*

Santa Cruz has many bike paths and various trails around
town. Fortunately, mountain bikers can utilize these to access
mountain bike rides from town. The popular routes are
described below.

Ride 31
West Cliff Path

Location: West Cliff Drive in Santa Cruz.

Distance: 2.7 miles one-way.

Elevation: 15/35 ft.

Trail Surface: 100% paved path.

Terrain: West Cliff Drive; ocean; cliffs; surf.

Technical Level: Easy.

Exertion Level: Mild.

*Looking across Cowell Beach surf break at the wharf and
the Beach Boardwalk from West Cliff Path.*

Highlights: Winding along the ocean cliffs from Cowell Beach to Natural Bridges State Park, this is simply the most popular bike path in Santa Cruz County.   Surfers, sea lions, inline skaters, whales, hippies, crashing waves, natural bridges, sunsets, a historic lighthouse and a surfing museum …this is where the action is.

Options: West Cliff is an excellent family ride in and of itself. This can also be connected with the Highway 1 Access Path (Ride 32) and the San Lorenzo Riverway (Ride 34) to combine for longer rides.

Note: There may be lots and lots and lots of people!

Directions/Access: Take Highway 1 (Mission St) north through town. Go left on Bay Street and continue until it ends at West Cliff Drive. The east end of the West Cliff Path is just above Cowell Beach and begins at the junction of Bay Street and West Cliff Drive. It follows the beach cliffs to Natural Bridges State Beach.

Ride 32
Highway 1 Access Path:
To Wilder Ranch

Location: Between Santa Cruz and Wilder Ranch.

Distance: 1.4 miles one-way.

Elevation: 40/90 ft.

Trail Surface: 100% paved path.

Terrain: Parallels the coastal side of Highway 1 far enough away from the noise of speeding traffic.

Technical Level: Easy.

Exertion Level: Mild.

Highlights: This paved access trail, part of the "County Bike Path," is a great way to get to Wilder Ranch from town or from the West Cliff Path, and makes a nice, easy, and safe family ride. Check out the BMX track off to the side (if it still exists)!

Options: Combine with Wilder Ranch/UCSC loop rides.

Note: Heavily utilized path on weekends!

Directions/Access: From Santa Cruz, take Highway 1 North (Mission St). Just as you are getting out of town, turn left on Shaffer Road (just past Western Dr) and park on the immediate right in the dirt parking area. Alternative (and safer) parking is on the other side of Highway 1 on Grand View Street.

Highway 1 Access Path. stretches from Wilder Ranch nearly to West Cliff Path.

Ride 33
Arroyo Seco Canyon Path

Location: North end of Santa Cruz, off Grand View St.

Distance: 1.1 miles one-way.

Elevation: 70/260 ft.

Trail Surface: 19% singletrack; 45% fire road; 36% paved path.

Terrain: Shady canyon; eucalyptus trees; creek.

Technical Level: Easy.

Exertion Level: Moderate; somewhat steep in parts.

Highlights: While it's a short trail, Arroyo Seco is a pretty canyon filled with eucalyptus and sometimes flowing water. The trail varies from singletrack to dirt and paved road. This is an excellent and uncrowded way to ride to UCSC from town.

Options: The trail can be connected to West Cliff Path, Highway 1 Access Path, Wilder Ranch, and UCSC. See Ride 9.

Note: Look out for both blackberry bushes and poison oak.

Directions/Access: For the southern access; follow Highway 1 (Mission St) north through town. Turn right on Swift St and veer left onto Grand View St. After the first stop sign, there is a small park with a playground a couple hundred feet up on the right. Spot the trail between a stucco wall and a chain link fence to the right of the park. The north end of the trail is off of Meder St in the University Terrace Park.

Ride 34
San Lorenzo Riverway

Location: Downtown Santa Cruz.

Elevation: 0/25 ft.

Distance: 3.9 miles total.

Trail Surface: 100% paved path.

Terrain: San Lorenzo River; downtown; boardwalk.

Technical Level: Easy.

Exertion Level: Mild.

Highlights: The San Lorenzo Riverway is the safest and most scenic way to bike through the city of Santa Cruz. It provides quick access between the beach areas and downtown.

Options: These bike paths can be combined with the other paths (Rides 31-33) to access the Wilder Ranch and UCSC trails.

Note: The path is not completely continuous; there are a couple places where you will need to cross a street.

Directions/Access: The bike path extends along both banks of the San Lorenzo River from Highway 1 to the Beach Boardwalk. Access is attainable virtually anywhere along the path. The inland-side paths are off Felker St (off of Ocean St) and the shopping center off River Street/Highway 1. Beach access is from the trestle off of East Cliff Dr or the east end of the Beach Boardwalk.

Keeping up with the ocean breezes.

Other Paths and Trails

Branciforte Creek Corridor Path
Following Branciforte Creek, this bike path can be used to access the downtown area bike paths with DeLaveaga Park. The south end of the path starts on Maye Ave off of Soquel Ave, about a block from San Lorenzo Riverway. It ends, after almost a mile, at Market St, a block from Highway 1.

Bay Street Bike Path
Surrounded by trees, a creek, and small pools, this path is actually located between the two sides of Bay St. It extends from Escalona Dr to Nobel Dr for about a mile, just before UCSC. Without a doubt, it is a safer and more pleasurable alternative than riding up Bay St to UCSC.

UCSC Bike Paths
UCSC has divided bike paths that bisect the sunny grassland area of the lower campus. Each side is approximately 1 mile long. The well-marked paths start at the first intersection off of Coolidge Dr (the continuation of Bay St) near the "farm area." Heading northwest, the bike paths end at the Music Center off Meyer St. To continue onto the North Campus trails, take Meyer St to Heller St, and go north.

Arana Gulch Trail
While this trail is only a half-mile long, it cuts from the upper Santa Cruz Harbor almost all the way to Soquel Ave. This quick access to the beach areas follows Arana Creek, through open meadows and oak woodland. The north entrance is located off Agnes St, which is off of Park Way on Soquel Ave (just west of Capitola Ave).

New Brighton Trails
New Brighton State Beach includes a couple miles of minor

trails in the open meadow areas. This is certainly not a biking destination, but some people ride around the area. From Park Ave Exit off Highway 1, go toward the beach. Turn left on McGregor Drive and right on New Brighton Road. Spot the trails by the gate on the left.

Coastal Rail Trail
The Coastal Rail Trail will be a bicycle and pedestrian path stretching all the way from Davenport to Watsonville. This is a much anticipated project in progress which will provide continual access along the Santa Cruz coast. The path will be constructed in segments over the next 5-10 years. More information can be found at www.sccrtc.org/pdf/railtrailfax.pdf.

Messing around in the Long Ridge Open Space Reserve.

Camping

New Brighton State Beach
Located 4 miles south of Santa Cruz, New Brighton State Beach features picnic areas, swimming, fishing, a nearby oak and pine forest, and developed campsites. Best of all, it is located just 1 mile from great mountain biking at the Forest of Nisene Marks. Reservations are highly recommended, especially during the summer. The beach can be reached by taking the New Brighton/Park Avenue exit off Highway 1. 831.464.6330

Seacliff State Beach
Seacliff State Beach has trailer/motorhome sites only, and is about 5 miles south of Santa Cruz. The beach is known for its fishing pier, cement ship, and a popular swimming spot. It has a covered picnic facility and an interpretive center as well. It also is a short ride to the trails of the Forest of Nisene Marks. Take the State Park Dr exit from Highway 1 in Aptos. Reservations are recommended! 831.429.2850

Manresa State Beach
About 12 miles south of Santa Cruz, Manresa State Beach features a beautiful expanse of sea and sand, with great fishing and surfing. Containing 64 tent-camping sites, RV's are not permitted. From Highway 1, south of Aptos, San Andreas Road heads southwest and continues for a few miles to Manresa, the first beach access upon reaching the coast. 831.761.1795/831.429.2850

Santa Cruz KOA (Kampgrounds-of-America)
This privately owned campground is for RV's, tents, and also has cabins. Near Manresa State Beach on San Andreas Road, the KOA has a heated pool, hot tub, mini-golf and bike rentals. 831.722.0551

Sunset State Beach
Sunset State Beach has developed campsites with pine trees, agricultural fields, sand dunes, and ocean side picnic spots. The beach is 16 miles south of Santa Cruz via Highway 1 and San Andreas Road. Reservations are recommended in summer! 831.763.7062

Big Basin State Park
Along with good mountain biking, Big Basin has fully developed campsites nestled in the redwoods. The park is 25 miles northwest of Santa Cruz via Highway 9. In Boulder Creek turn left on Highway 236 for about 9 miles. There are also walk-in/bike-in camps along the Skyline to Sea Trail near Waddell Creek. The parking for this area is about 12 miles north of Santa Cruz on Highway 1. 831.338.8860

Henry Cowell Redwoods State Park
At Henry Cowell, you can jump on the mountain bike trails directly from your campsite, which link to Pogonip, UCSC, and Wilder Ranch. There are 113 developed campsites with $1 bike-in camping. Make reservations on the weekends and during prime summer months. The campground is closed in the winter. From Santa Cruz, take Graham Hill Road (off Ocean Street) about 4 miles; the campground is on the left. 831.438.2396

Playing on a see-saw in the Santa Cruz forest.

The Forest of Nisene Marks State Park
Tent camping, picnic tables and barbecue pits are available for walk-in, or bike-in tent camping only. The trail camp is located six miles from the nearest parking lot. Call for a camping permit. 831.763.7062

Castle Rock State Park
Located north of Big Basin near Saratoga Gap, Castle Rock State Park's campground is on Highway 35 (Skyline Blvd), just 2 1/2 miles southeast of the junction with Highway 9. While mountain biking is not allowed, the park is known for hiking and rock climbing. 408.867.2952

There's something sick and twisted about this trail.

Resources

IMBA
www.imba.com
The head honcho for mountain bike advocacy.

MBOSC (Mountain Bikers of Santa Cruz)
www.mbosc.org
The main Santa Cruz mountain bike and advocacy group.

ROMP (Responsibly Organized Mountain Peddlers)
www.romp.org

Group promoting mountain cycling advocacy and social events in southwest Bay Area.

Team Wrong Way
www.teamwrongway.com
Bay Area racing organization.

Trailworkers.com
www.trailworkers.com
Santa Cruz county trail work organization.

Friends of Santa Cruz State Parks
www.scparkfriends.org
Dedicated to the long-term preservation of local State Park resources.

Northern California / Nevada Cycling Association
www.ncnca.org/mtn.html
Northern California/Nevada mountain biking events.

Santa Cruz County Visitor Center & Information
www.santacruzca.org
1211 Ocean St. Santa Cruz, CA
800.833.3494
831.425.1234

Santa Cruz Parks & Recreation
www.santacruzparksandrec.com
323 Church St. Santa Cruz, CA 95060
831.420.5270

Santa Cruz State Parks
www.SantaCruzStateParks.org

California State Parks
www.parks.ca.gov

Mountain Bike Events

Please check the websites listed below for updated information on ever-changing local events:

Surf City Cyclocross; Watsonville
www.cyclo-x.com
Multiple events in the fall and winter.

Sea Otter Classic; Monterey
www.seaotterclassic.com
One of the biggest mountain bike events in the West, usually held in the spring.

**Central Coast Cycling Mountain Bike Series
& Cyclo-Cross;** Santa Cruz area
www.cccx.org
NCNCA Sanctioned local events throughout the winter.

Boggs Mountain Bash; Boggs Mountain
www.csmevents.com
Usually in the spring/summer.

24-Hours of Adrenalin; Monterey
www.24hoursofadrenalin.com
NORBA sanctioned event in spring/summer.

Groovy Gravity Games; Livermore
www.teamwrongway.com
Downhill event in the spring.

Women's Mtn Bike Rally; Wilder Ranch
www.csmevents.com
An all-women's race in the summer.

The Sizzler Classic; San Jose
www.csmevents.com
Cross country event in spring/summer.

Ride Series; Hollister
www.purejuice.net
NORBA sanctioned events in the winter.

Racin' at the Ranch; Gilroy
www.purejuice.net
NORBA sanctioned race on a private ranch in the fall.

For more up-to-date information on local races, see
www.wrongway.com and www.csmevents.com.

Spicing up the Old Cove/Ohlone Bluffs Ride (Ride 1).

Bike Shops

Another Bike Shop
2361 Mission St; Santa Cruz; 831.427.2232

Sprockets
1420 Mission St; Santa Cruz; 831.426.7623

Bicycle Shop
1325 Mission St; Santa Cruz; 831.454.0909

Armadillo Cyclery
1211 Mission St; Santa Cruz; 831.426.7299

Bike Coop
1156 High St; Santa Cruz; 831.457.8281

Spokesman Bicycles
231 Cathcart St; Santa Cruz; 831.423.LOVE

Dave's Bike Shop
318 Pacific Ave; Santa Cruz; 831.423.8923

The Bicycle Trip
1127 Soquel Ave; Santa Cruz; 831.427.2580

Bill's Bike Repair
2628 Soquel Ave; Santa Cruz; 831.477.0511

Recycled Bikes of Santa Cruz
2420 7th Ave; Santa Cruz; 831.465.9955

Cruiser King
575-A 7th Ave; Santa Cruz; 831.477.1288

Cycle Works
1203 41st Ave; Capitola; 831.476.7092

Family Cycling Center
 914 41st Ave; Capitola; 831.475.3883

Aptos Bike Trail
7514 Soquel Dr; Aptos; 831.688.8650

Mr E's Cyclery
8059 Aptos St; Aptos; 831.662.2973

Scotts Valley Cycle Sport
245-J Mount Hermon Rd; Scotts Valley; 831.440.9070

Trey's True Wheels
1431 Main St; Watsonville; 831.786.0200

Mountain biking in Santa Cruz.

Index of Rides By Category

Sweet Singletrack
(rides may contain some non-singletrack sections)

Ride 4   Wilder Singletrack Loop
Ride 2   Wilder Ridge Loop
Ride 18   Vienna Woods Combo Loop
Ride 17   Aptos Rancho Trail
Ride 23   Outer Demo Loop
Ride 24   Inner Demo Loop
Ride 3   Baldwin/Enchanted Loop
Ride 15   Top of the World Loop
Ride 16   Figure 8 Loop
Ride 29   Saratoga Gap Trail
Ride 30   Long Ridge Loop
Ride 11   U-Con Trail

Mellow Cruisers

Ride 1   Old Cove Landing/Ohlone Bluff Trail
Ride 26   Waddell Creek/Skyline to the Sea Trail
Ride 19   Aptos Creek Fire Road: to Porter Picnic area
Ride 31   West Cliff Bike Path

Technical Tests

Ride 23   Outer Demo Loop
Ride 24   Inner Demo Loop
Ride 15   Top of the World Loop (depending on spur
options chosen)
Ride 4   Wilder Singletrack Loop
Ride 2   Wilder Ridge Loop

Hammerhead Climbs

Ride 22   Ultra Mega Nisene-Demo Ride
Ride 30   Long Ridge Loop (with the Grizzly Flat/Charcoal
          Road addition)
Ride 27   Big Basin Loop (with spur additions)

Ride 13   Redwoods to Coast Loop (loop/out & back)
Ride 19   Aptos Creek Fire Road with Ride 20 addition
Ride 21   Hinckley Basin Fire Road with Ride 20 addition
Ride 24   Inner Demo Loop (double loop)
Ride 5   Wilder-Gray Whale Loop
Ride 9   Arroyo Seco-UCSC-Wilder Loop

Insane Downhills
(includes uphill pedaling as well)
Ride 15   Top of the World Loop
Ride 24   Inner Demo Loop
Ride 19   Aptos Creek Fire Road
Ride 27   Big Basin Loop
Ride 28A   Gazos Creek Road (one way shuttle)
Ride 2   Wilder Ridge Loop
Ride 5   Wilder-Gray Whale Loop

Epic Big-Day Rides
Ride 22   Ultra Mega Nisene-Demo Ride
Ride 13   Redwoods to Coast Ride (loop option)
Ride 27   Big Basin Loop (with spur trail exploration)

Multi Interest Rides
Rides 1-6 All Wilder Ranch Rides; (Cultural Preserve)
Ride 5   Wilder Gray Whale Loop; (lime kiln, quarry)
Ride 1   Old Cove/Ohlone Bluff Trail;
           (natural bridges & marine life)
Ride 26   Waddell Creek/Skyline to Sea Trail;
           (hike to waterfall)
Ride 27   Big Basin Loop;
           (redwoods, ocean and mountain views)
Ride 12   Henry Cowell Loop; (observation tower, San
           Lorenzo River, redwoods)
Ride 15   Top of the World Loop; (disc golf)
Ride 30   Long Ridge Loop; (panoramic ocean & mountain
           views; rock climbing in the area)

Ride 19   Aptos Creek Fire Road; (Loma Prieta Earthquake
            Center; hikes to waterfalls, logging & mill sites).

Quick Fixes
Ride 18   Vienna Woods Combo Loop
Ride 17   Aptos Rancho Trail
Ride 15   Top of the World Loop
Ride 16   Figure 8 Loop
Ride 11   U-Con Trail
Ride 7   North Campus Loop
Ride 21   Hinckley Basin Fire Road

Multi-Park/ Interregional Rides
Ride 22   Ultra Mega Nisene-Demo Ride
Ride 9   Arroyo Seco-UCSC-Wilder Loop
Ride 8   Cowell-Wilder Regional Trail
Ride 13   Redwoods to Coast Ride
Ride 30   Long Ridge Loop

Santa Cruz Classics
Ride 2   Wilder Ridge Loop
Ride 4   Wilder Singletrack Loop
Ride 15   Top of the World Loop with Figure 8 Loop
Ride 1   Old Cove Landing/Ohlone Bluff Trail
Ride 23   Outer Demo Loop (or Inner Demo Loop)
Ride 19   Aptos Creek Fire Road
Ride 26   Waddel Creek/Skyline to the Sea Trail

Index of Trails and Rides

Index of Maps

Special Thanks

Thanks to all our friends and family that helped with creating this book! Big loud Thank You's go out to Jay and Kira Brown, Allison Bell, Jon Diller, and Jeff Block for helping with the rides and pictures! Jay, thanks sooo much for all the posing (don't worry, you're not a poser).

We appreciate the editing help from the Block family and the endless support from all the Dillers. We are also grateful for help from Randall Cornish and John Moynier.

Super special thanks to Rob Roskopp and Santa Cruz Bicycles for providing the insane bikes!

About The Authors

Dave Diller has spent most of his life in Santa Cruz. In 1983, he starting mountain biking Nisene Marks and other Santa Cruz areas. In addition to mountain biking, he loves motocross, surfing, snowboarding, and basically anything out-doors. Dave went to Soquel High School and graduated from the University of California Santa Cruz.

Allison Diller has lived all over the country and eventually found herself back in Santa Cruz riding mountain bikes. When not riding, she loves playing beach volleyball, surfing, and adventuring around with husband Dave. She graduated from Harbor High School and University of California Santa Barbara.

Productions

If you have any questions, suggestions, or corrections, please email them to info@extremeline.com.

Look for the upcoming mountain biking guidebooks from Extremeline Productions:

Mountain Biking Mammoth
ISBN 0-9723361-1-7

Mountain Biking Santa Barbara
ISBN 0-9723361-2-5

Additional copies of *Mountain Biking Santa Cruz* can be ordered at www.extremeline.com. For more information on purchasing books, email orders@extremeline.com.

WWW.EXTREMELINE.COM